IMAGES
of America

NASHVILLE
BREWING

ON THE COVER: The photograph on the cover of this book is of the Silver Dollar Saloon from around the early 1900s. The saloon was located in the V. E. Schwab building on the corner of Broad and Market Streets in the heart of downtown Nashville. The building still stands today and is used as the gift shop for Nashville's Hard Rock Café on what is now the corner of Broadway and Second Avenue. (From the collection of the Tennessee State Library and Archives.)

IMAGES
of America

NASHVILLE
BREWING

Scott R. Mertie
with forewords by Patricia Gerst Benson
and John J. Gerst Sr.

ARCADIA
PUBLISHING

Published by Arcadia Publishing
Charleston, South Carolina

Library of Congress Catalog Card Number: 2006929821

For all general information contact Arcadia Publishing at:
Telephone 843-853-2070
Fax 843-853-0044
E-mail sales@arcadiapublishing.com
For customer service and orders:
Toll-Free 1-888-313-2665

Visit us on the Internet at www.arcadiapublishing.com

Three young women pose for a picture in from of a Gerst Beer and Ale billboard. "Brewed In Dixie," which was a popular advertising slogan used by the Brewery in the 1940s, can be seen at the bottom of the billboard. (From the collection of Scott R. Mertie.)

CONTENTS

ACKNOWLEDGMENTS

There are a number of people who provided invaluable help during the process of writing this book, and I will try to list them all here.

First I have to start out by thanking my parents, as without them, I probably never would have starting collecting beer cans and developed an interest in brewery history. My mom took my Cub Scout troop on a tour of the Anheuser-Busch brewery, and my father would bring me back beer cans from his international business trips. As a family, we went to some of the country's first brewpubs and microbreweries during my teenage years. I can honestly say they are not the average set of parents.

I need to recognize the following friends and fellow collectors who helped contribute to this book: Shawn Cunningham, of the Goldcrest 51 collectibles club, for giving me his continuous support during this endeavor; John Boertlein and Kip Sharp offered their superb research materials; Norman Jay, Sam Hunt, and Terry Williams all provided photographs of their impressive collections; and Kimberly Holn, bar manager of the Gerst Haus, for putting up with my constant requests for photographing the interior of the restaurant.

The following people and organizations provided informative historical data and photographs for this book: Beth Odle and the Nashville Room staff of the Tennessee State Library, Karina McDaniel and the staff of the Tennessee State Library and Archives, Laura Carrillo and the staff at the Parthenon, Metropolitan Archives for Nashville and Davidson County, Elizabeth Dunham of the University of Tennessee Special Collections Library, and Randy Carlson of Carlson's Brewery Research.

Also I can't offer enough gratitude to Pat Benson, Jack Gerst, and Walter Diehl for allowing me to inquire into their family's personal history and for providing their family photographs and stories. I also need to thank Maggie Bullwinkel, acquisitions editor, and the rest of the team at Arcadia Publishing for assisting me through the writing, editing, and publishing process.

Finally I must thank my wife and best friend, Candy. Without her support and encouragement, this book would not have been possible. She has been the wind in my sails and bestowed me with her unconditional love; therefore I dedicate this book to her.

FOREWORD
BY PATRICIA GERST BENSON

When William Gerst, my great-grandfather, arrived in Cincinnati in 1866 from his home in Alpirsback, Germany, little did he realize the impact this voyage would have in fulfilling his dreams to study the art of brewing, nor could he have imagined the economic stability his brewing interest would bring to the city of Nashville. At one time the company produced 200,000 barrels of beer annually and employed hundreds of people.

A man of varied interest, William Gerst pursued his love of horse racing and breeding on his farm in Hermitage, near Nashville, Tennessee. On May 10, 1910, this passion paid off with a winner of the Kentucky Derby. Donau, his bay colt Thoroughbred, carried the Gerst colors of red, white, and blue to victory in the 36th running of the derby. To this date, his horse has been the only horse owned by a Tennessean to win this respected race at Churchill Downs.

When I was in my teens, I developed a special friendship with my grandmother, Elizabeth Schneider Gerst, the wife of August Gerst, son of William Gerst. I recall with great fondness her many stories of life at Gerst camp where the men fished, hunted, and played cards until the wee hours. She and her sister, Josie, who married Albert Gerst, provided authentic German dishes for these occasions, some of which are still listed on the menu of the Gerst Haus restaurant.

It has been over 100 years since that voyage my great-grandfather took, and there is still an interest in his life, times, and vocation. Antique shops and the Internet are frequented by many people searching for Gerst memorabilia and that link to the past. It is with great appreciation that I applaud the efforts of historians such as Scott R. Mertie for preserving the memories and facts of this area. It is from the past that we strive to make a better future for our generations.

—Patricia Gerst Benson
Chocowinity, North Carolina

FOREWORD

BY JOHN J. GERST SR.

William Gerst is my fourth cousin, twice removed. Our families were originally from the town of Balingen, which is located in Schwarzwaldkreis, Wurttemberg, Germany. The Gerst name is considered to be of Swabia (German Schwaben, Latin Suevia) origin. Swabia, with its (former) capital at Augsburg, was a medieval duchy in the lands now forming southwestern Germany. The term Swabia nowadays is used in a more restricted way and does not refer to the whole area once encompassed by medieval duchy. It is related to the custom of speaking Swabian dialect, which is prevailing on the territory of Wurttemberg, in the area of the Danube (till the Lake Constance, or Bodensee, and the Rhine) called Oberschwaben and the region between Iller and Lech, called Bavarian Swabia.

William's grandfather, Johannes Gerst, immigrated to the town of Alpirsbach in or about 1910. Later Johannes Gerst married Frederika Roth on February 2, 1814, in Alpirsbach.

Patricia Gerst Benson and I have corresponded over the years, and we have been sharing many family pictures and records pertaining to the Gerst family history. We are sixth cousins, once removed. Scott R. Mertie contacted Patricia because he was writing a book about the history of the William Gerst Brewing Company located in Nashville, Tennessee. Since I was very successful in researching the Gerst family in the United States and Germany, she recommended that Scott contact me in order to provide him with some valuable documentation.

We commend Scott R. Mertie for wanting to preserve our family's brewing history in text for future generations to read and enjoy. At the present time, it should be noted that members of the Gerst family can still be found living in the towns of Alpirsbach, Balingen, and Stuttgart.

—Jack Gerst
Marlton, New Jersey

INTRODUCTION

From the ancient Samarians fermenting bread to make ninkasi, to chicha being made high up in the Andes, to the rice beers of the orient, to the European ales of the middle ages, beer has been a part of human civilization for thousands of years. German, Irish, and other European immigrants brought their customs and traditions with them to the United States, along with their rich brewing knowledge.

Jumping forward to the mid-1800s, the brewing industry was just starting to develop in the southern part of the United States. Many German families immigrated to Nashville during this period, as Nashville was a booming river city, and jobs were prevalent for skilled laborers.

Nashville's first brewery began operations in 1859 but quickly ceased production two years later due to the Civil War. Once the war ended in 1865, several breweries started to begin brewing beer in downtown Nashville. These breweries kegged their beer and delivered it by horse and wagon to saloons nearby. Several other wholesalers would receive large barrels of beer by rail from breweries in the Midwest to be kegged and bottled on-site.

By 1890, there was only one brewery left in town. This was operated by William Gerst and his decedents for the next 64 years. The brewery saw many highs during its existence in Nashville, such as winning the gold medal for its beer at the 1897 Tennessee Centennial Exposition; Gerst's racehorse, Donau, winning the Kentucky Derby in 1910; and the successful advertising campaign for its 50th anniversary celebration in 1940.

Unfortunately, there were many lows that the brewery encountered as well. The Temperance Movement and later Prohibition nearly doomed brewery in the early 1900s. Later the national breweries with large advertising budgets and refrigerated rail cars forced the closing of the brewery in 1954.

During the first half of the 20th century, the William Gerst Brewing Company was one of the largest breweries in the South. The brewery kegged, bottled, and even canned their various brands of beer for consumers throughout the southern states.

The William Gerst Brewery Company closed in 1954 due to national competition, and beer was not made locally in Nashville for the next 34 years until Tennessee's first microbrewery opened in 1988. Since then, several other craft breweries have sprouted and provided the opportunity for Nashvillians to enjoy locally brewed beer.

AUTHOR'S NOTE: This book is intended to give a general overview of brewing in Nashville. It briefly touches on a lot of areas, but does focus mainly on the William Gerst Brewing Company, as this was the only operational brewery in Nashville for most of the 20th century. Because this book is only 128 pages, I was not able to get nearly as detailed as I would have liked on the Gerst family history, nor was I able to include images of every known piece of Nashville breweriana.

One

EARLY NASHVILLE
BREWING

The Nashville Brewery changed hands several times since it first opened in 1859. This artist's sketch appears as the only reference to Nashville brewing in the historical brewing reference book *One Hundred Years of Brewing*. The Nashville Brewery started as a small brewery built by Jacob Stifel located on the corner of Mulberry and South High Streets. It changed hands several times over the next 30 years until finally becoming the William Gerst Brewing Company in 1893. Other early Nashville breweries included McMormack and Company, E. Ottenville, W. Beaty, Crossman and Drucker, City Brewery, and the Union Brewery. (From the collection of Scott R. Mertie.)

Malachi McCormack starting brewing in Nashville in 1859 but moved to Louisville once the Civil War started in 1861. After the war, he moved back to Nashville and was operating the M. McCormack and Company brewery by 1871 at 105 Cherry Street. In 1872, McCormack had partnered with Eugene Ottenville, where they bottled under the name E. O. McCormack. The clear bottle shown on the left is from the M. McCormack and Company brewery, and the amber bottle is from E. O. McCormack. (From the collection of Terry Williams.)

Several years later, in 1875, Ottenville opened his own brewery where he operated under his own name until it closed in the mid-1880s. McCormack brought on another partner named McKee and brewed as McCormack and McKee for only one year. The bottle pictured on the left is from McCormack and McKee, while the two bottles on the right are from Ottenville. (From the collection of Terry Williams.)

Adam Diehl and George Lord formed a company in 1868 to distribute kegged and bottled beer from various midwestern breweries and water from Tennessee springs. In 1884, Diehl and Lord built this modern, three-story brick building on the corner of Front and•Church Streets, where the Beer Sellar bar is located today. Such brands transported from the North include Lemp's and Budweiser from St. Louis, Schlitz from Milwaukee, Lion from Cincinnati, and Cook's from Evansville. (From the collection of the Nashville Room, Tennessee Public Library.)

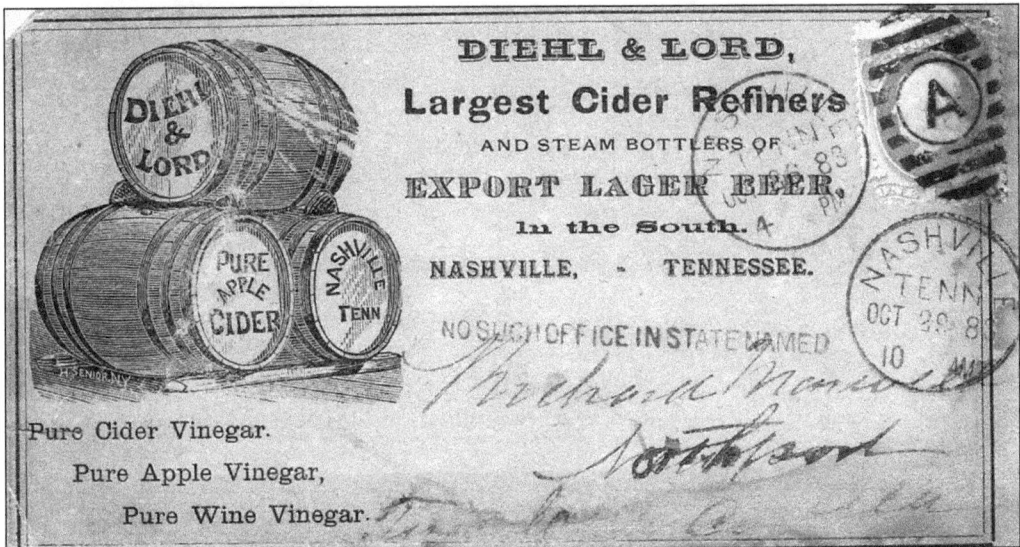

In addition to beer, Diehl and Lord also bottled cider and sparkling water, among other beverages. This postcard, postmarked October 29, 1883, boasts that it's the South's largest refiner of cider and steam bottlers for export lager beer. During this time, Diehl and Lord employed 50 people at the facility and other salesmen throughout the South. (From the collection of Walter Diehl.)

Early Diehl and Lord bottles included such varieties as blob-top sodas and Hutchinson's, as well as crock, blob top, and squat ale bottles. Many of these bottles are found throughout Nashville during demolitions and new construction digs. (From the collection of Terry Williams.)

The bottling area inside of the Diehl and Lord facility shows a huge production facility that was 100 feet by 120 feet. George Lord moved to Memphis to manage their other facility in 1878 and later retired in 1889. Adam Diehl continued to operate the company at several Nashville locations until he died in 1925. The business continued to operate until 1928, when it permanently closed, never seeing the end of Prohibition. (From the collection of the Nashville Room, Tennessee Public Library.)

James E. Hays was the sole proprietor for a beer distributing company located on the corner of Market and Gay Streets. This company was originally formed by E. Ottenville in 1875 and later became the Nashville Beer and Bottling Company before it was purchased by Hays in the 1890s. By the early 1900s, the Hays facility employed six wagons to distribute beer and was able to hold cold storage for 10 rail cars full of beer barrels. (From the collection of the Nashville Room, Tennessee Public Library.)

JAMES E. HAYS,

AGENT FOR

John Hauck Brewing Company's Celebrated

Cincinnati Beer

AND
Pabst Milwaukee Export and Select Bottled Beers.

Telephone 1489.

CORNER MARKET AND GAY STREETS

James Hays was in the wholesale business and was the sole agent for the John Hauck Brewing Company of Cincinnati and the Pabst Brewing Company of Milwaukee. This advertisement was in the St. Mary's Cathedral souvenir brochure from Tennessee's Centennial Exposition in 1897. (From the collection of Scott R. Mertie.)

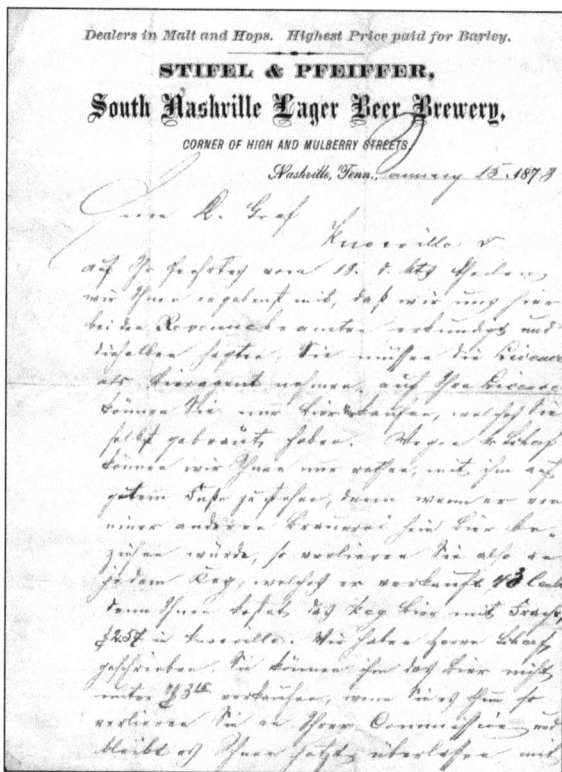

Dealers in Malt and Hops. Highest Price paid for Barley.

STIFEL & PFEIFFER,

South Nashville Lager Beer Brewery,

CORNER OF HIGH AND MULBERRY STREETS,

Nashville, Tenn. January 15, 1873

[letter handwritten in Old German]

After the Civil War, Jacob Stifel started the Nashville Brewery on the location that would eventually become the William Gerst Brewing Company. In 1863, Stifel partnered with a Mr. Pfeiffer, and together they operated the brewery until it was auctioned to J. B. Kuhn on November 16, 1876. This letterhead from January 15, 1873, is written in Old German to beer distributors in Knoxville and discusses the prices for various jugs of beer. The letter also indicates that Stifel included a bag of celery and radishes with the shipment of beer for the distributor to enjoy. (From the collection of the University of Tennessee Special Collections Library.)

After purchasing the concern, J. B. Kuhn changed the name to the South Nashville Ale and Lager Beer Brewery. He only owned the brewery for two years when he sold it to C. A. Maus and Brothers in 1878. Two years later, the brewery was sold again to John Burkhardt and a Mr. Herschel, who changed the name to the Nashville Brewing Company. (From the collection of the Nashville Room, Tennessee Public Library.)

16

Burkhardt and Herschel only held the Nashville Brewing Company for two years when they sold it to brothers William and Archibald Walker in 1882. This picture from the mid-1880s shows the daily operations of the Nashville Brewing Company. Wood kegs are loaded on horse-drawn wagons to be delivered to local taverns and saloons. (From the collection of the Tennessee State Library and Archives.)

WILLIAM WALKER.   ARCHIBALD WALKER,

NASHVILLE BREWING CO.,

WM. & ARCH'D WALKER, Proprietors.,

BREWERS OF

PILSENER AND LAGER BEER,

OFFICE & BREWERY, COR. HIGH & MULBERRY STS.,

Telephone No- 393.   NASHVILLE, TENN.

This clipping from the 1885 Nashville City Directory lists William and Archibald Walker as proprietors and brewers of the Nashville Brewing Company. The brothers focused on pilsner and lager beers, which were growing in popularity in Nashville as well as throughout the United States. The Walkers operated the brewery until it was sold to two Cincinnati brewers in 1890. (From the collection of the Nashville and Davidson County Archives.)

The Nashville Brewing Company was purchased by Christian Moerlein and William Gerst in 1890. As this 1890 Nashville City Directory reflects, the brewery's name was changed to the Moerlein-Gerst Brewing Company. This city directory also lists the Diehl and Lord Steam Bottling Works. (From the collection of Terry Williams.)

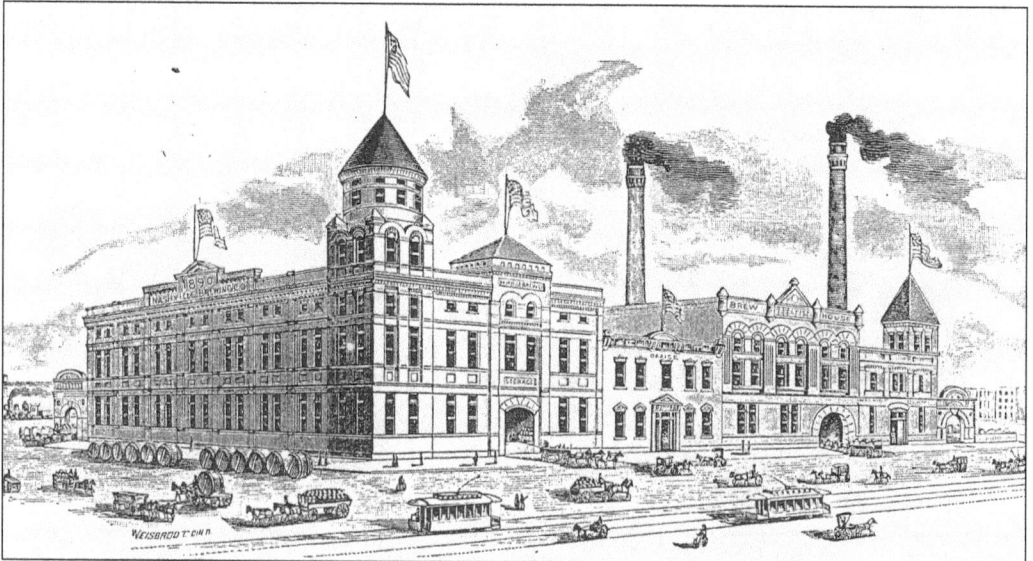

This sketch shows the Moerlein-Gerst Brewing Company in the early 1890s after a significant expansion was made to the existing Nashville Brewing Company. The exaggerated drawing of the expanded brewer was made in Cincinnati by a Mr. Weisbrodt and was used to promote the brewery for years to come. (From the collection of the Nashville Room, Tennessee Public Library.)

Christian Moerlein operated the hugely successful Christian Moerlein Brewing Company in Cincinnati. Moerlein was able to finance the purchase of the Nashville Brewing Company and invest enormous amounts of capital to expand it. Moerlein never moved to Nashville. Instead he sent his longtime brewmaster, William Gerst, to Nashville to brew and oversee operations. (From the collection of the Nashville and Davidson County Archives.)

Gerst came from a long line of brewers from the Bavaria region of Germany. He was born on June 28, 1847, in Alpirsbach. He grew up in the brewery business and immigrated to the United States in 1866 at the age of 19. Gerst settled in Cincinnati, Ohio, and gained employment at the Christian Moerlein Brewing Company. Gerst knew how to operate a large brewery, yet he was also was able to deal with people. In the early 1880s, he was instrumental in the brewing industry by replacing striking union laborers. Ironically, the William Gerst Brewing Company would later boast that its beer was union made. (From the collection of the Nashville Room, Tennessee Public Library.)

The first brands of beer brewed by the Moerlein-Gerst Brewing Company were Old Jug Lager and Pilsener Export. Both of these brands continued to be brewed, in some form or fashion, under the Gerst name for the next 50 years. The brewery poster advertises that Moerlein-Gerst has the finest keg lager in the world. (From the collection of Scott R. Mertie.)

Pictured are three early examples of crocks used to bottle Old Jug Lager, a popular brand distributed by the Moerlein-Gerst Brewing Company. The crocks were produced in Glasgow, Scotland, and were simultaneously used by Christian Moerlein in Cincinnati. The crocks contained brilliant graphics with a cherub and the statement that Old Jug Lager is "the fashionable beverage of the day, brilliant in colds, absolutely pure, stimulating, and rejuvenating, fully matured, a veritable luxury." The crock on the right contains the Tennessee agricultural shield, while the other two have a rooster as their logo. The rooster was believed to be a European culinary symbol and was often associated with food and beverage advertising in the 19th century. (From the collection of Scott R. Mertie.)

These Moerlein-Gerst Brewing Company embossed blob-top bottles were found several years ago when ground was broken for the new Nashville Symphony. Blob-top bottles were made by wrapping a piece of molten glass around the top of the blown bottle. Once cooled, the blob-top would act as a support for the cork, since bottle caps had not yet been invented. (From the collection of Terry Williams.)

This is the first of many advertising lithographs to be issued by the brewery. This is however the only one known to exist that was issued under the Moerlein-Gerst Brewing Company, rather than the William Gerst Brewing Company. The woman in the lithograph is believed to be a popular opera singer for this time period, although it is difficult to confirm. (From the collection of Norman Jay.)

The Moerlein-Gerst Brewing Company produced this 1891 souvenir for patrons of the opera *Last Days of Pompeii*. The card has vibrant colors and is approximately three inches by three inches. (From the collection of Terry Williams.)

Two

THE BEGINNING OF A BREWING EMPIRE

In March 1893, William Gerst purchased the controlling interest of the brewery from Christian Moerlein and renamed it the William Gerst Brewing Company. This is one of the very first advertisements issued under the brewery's new name. It boasted the massive brewery, new bottling house, and the brands of the day. (From the collection of Scott R. Mertie.)

William Gerst became a very prominent businessman in Nashville, but he was also a dedicated family man. He married Mary Kunigunda Engel in 1870, and they had six children: William Jr., born in 1870; Bertha, born in 1875; Emma, born in 1877, Albert, born 1884; George J., born in 1886; and August L., born in 1890. All of Gerst's sons would work at the brewery and eventually run the brewery upon his retirement. (From the collection of the Gerst Haus, Nashville, Tennessee.)

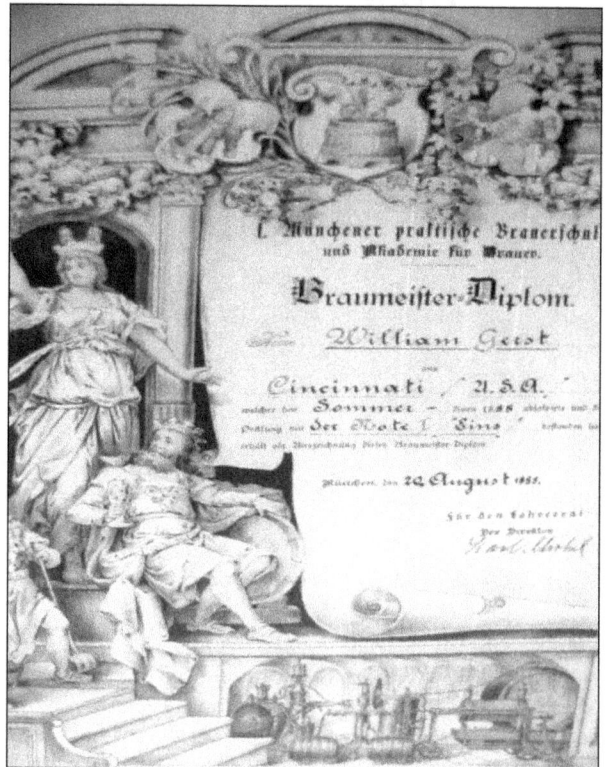

William Gerst received his master brewer's certificate on August 20, 1888, while he was working in Cincinnati. In 1889, Gerst was elected as the second president of the United States Brewmasters Association. In Nashville, he was an Elk and served on various community boards. (From the collection of the Gerst Haus, Nashville, Tennessee.)

Saloons were scattered throughout Nashville and were where the workingman would go to enjoy some Tennessee sippin' whiskey or a cold beer. This saloon from the 1890s contains several William Gerst Brewing Company advertisements in the windows and tin signs on either side of the door. Notice the dirt roads and horse harnesses near the entrance. (From the collection of Scott R. Mertie.)

Many of the pre-prohibition beers were bottled in embossed beer bottles. The two clear bottles above are blob tops and were probably issued in the late 1890s. The first one is a quart bottle, and the other one holds a pint. The bottles below represent two nice examples of the Gerst logo embossed in the glass. The first one is an amber quart blob-top, and the second is a clear bottle with a top that is more common in the 20th century. Both bottles held one quart of beer. (From the collection of Scott R. Mertie.)

This is the earliest known lithograph issued under the William Gerst Brewing Company name, which is dated 1894. Although difficult to confirm, it is believed the woman pictured in the lithograph is an opera singer who was popular during this period. This lithograph was shown at the William Gerst Brewing Company's display at the Tennessee Centennial Exposition in 1897. (From the collection of Sam Hunt.)

This colorful lithograph was also displayed at the Gerst exhibit during the Centennial Exposition, which dates the lithograph between 1893 and 1897. It was popular for breweries of the day to issue lithographs of woman to advertise their beer. Sometimes they are "stock models," and the same print can be seen in other parts of the country advertising another brewery. (From the collection of Norman Jay.)

Get a bottle of

Gerst

Beer

At the German Village

... See it bottled at our exhibit
Visit the Brewery and see it made

William Gerst realized that he could get involved with state fairs and other events where the public would be introduced to his beer. This advertisement indicates that the William Gerst Brewing Company has an exhibit at the German Village, which was at the Tennessee State Fair. It promotes its new bottling line and even points out that the beer can be seen bottled at the exhibit. Gerst adopted the dove within the G as his new logo, and it was used on brands throughout the brewery's life. (From the collection of Scott R. Mertie.)

..The..

William Gerst Brewing

Company,

NASHVILLE, TENNESSEE.

THE LARGEST AND BEST EQUIPPED BREWERY IN THE SOUTH.

PRODUCING ONLY

High Grade Draught and

Bottled Beer.

This ad for the William Gerst Brewing Company appeared in the souvenir program distributed by Nashville's St. Mary's Cathedral. It was printed just prior to the Tennessee Centennial Exposition in 1897 and covered the church's history from 1847 to the program's printing. It is interesting to note that the advertisement specifies that Gerst brews "special beers for family use." (From the collection of Scott R. Mertie.)

William Painter invented the crown bottle cap in 1892, but it was not widely used until the beginning of the 20th century. Prior to the crown, corks and other devises were used as stoppers. The William Gerst Brewing Company had this warning label of sorts on some of its advertising depicting that Gerst name must be on the cork in order to be genuine. This would ensure that other companies did not reuse the embossed bottles and claim it was Gerst's beer inside. Below is a corkscrew depicting the William Gerst Brewing Company's name on it. These were given to customers who bought bottled beer from the brewery. (From the collection of Scott R. Mertie.)

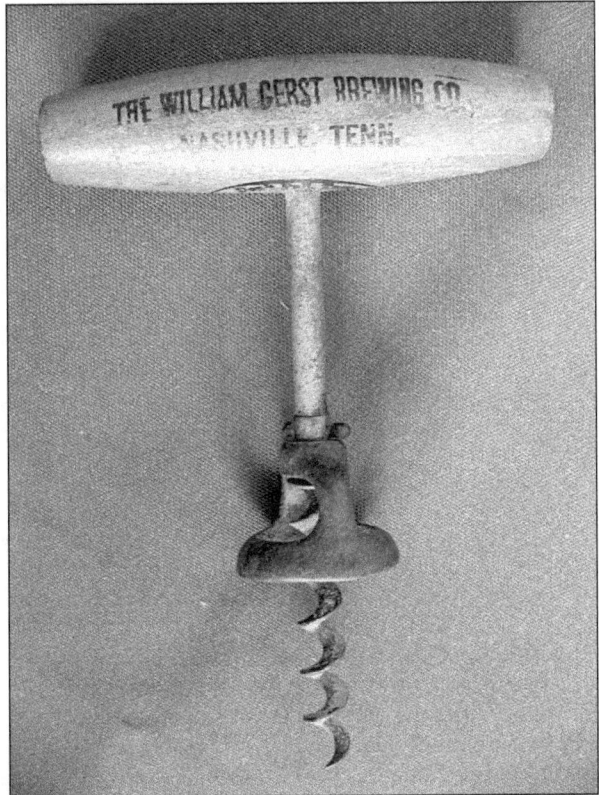

Tennessee celebrated its 100th anniversary as a state of the Union in 1897. To commemorate this historic birthday, the state decided to hold a large exposition during the fall of 1897. Planning and construction began the year prior, and many buildings were erected on the sight in West Nashville, which is now known as Centennial Park. Gerst was highly involved with the planning of the exposition and made sure that his beer was served at various concessions throughout. This Tennessee Centennial Program, from the week ending October 30, reflects the four restaurants where Gerst's beer can be enjoyed. (From the collection of Scott R. Mertie.)

This William Gerst Brewing Company advertisement for the Tennessee Centennial Exposition lists the varieties of beer that can be purchased. They included Pilsner, a traditional German lager; Extra Pale, a hoppy ale; and Bohemian, which was most likely a pilsner brewed in the style made popular by brewers in today's Czech Republic. (From the collection of Scott R. Mertie.)

Early on during the Tennessee Exposition, a competition was held to determine the best tasting beer in the South. Many breweries from Tennessee and abroad were represented, but the William Gerst Brewing Company was the only one that was locally brewed. Gerst won the gold medal at this event, and brewery employees can be seen here celebrating in a parade which stopped in front of the casino. (Courtesy of the Parthenon, Metro Parks.)

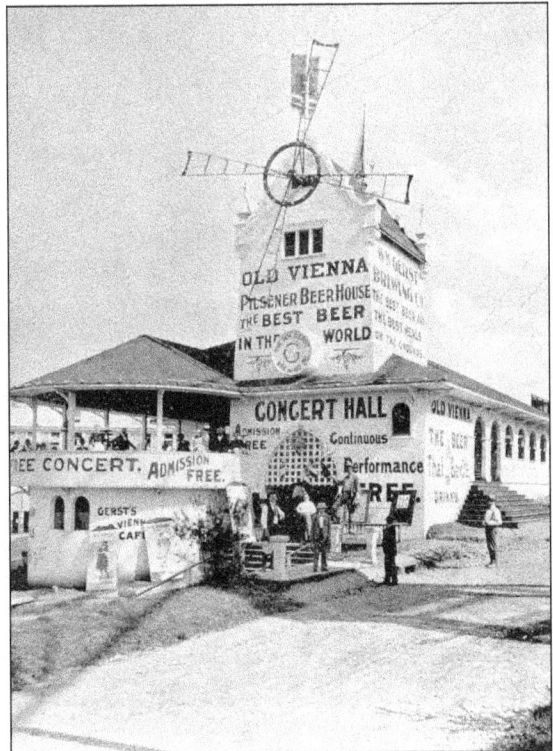

The Old Vienna Pilsner Beer House was a restaurant where exposition attendees could stop to get a bite to eat, listen to bands in the concert hall, and of course, cool off with some Gerst Beer. One wonders if some Bavarian recipes used at this restaurant are also used at the Gerst Haus restaurant, which opened up nearly 60 years later. "The beer that everyone drinks," and "the best beer in the world," were clearly advertised on the side of Old Vienna. (From the collection of the Parthenon, Metro Parks.)

The Café Militaire advertised the "largest kitchen with the coolest beers." This restaurant was designed with a military motif and offered the finest vaudeville performances in the South. Complete, full-course meals at Café Militaire were only 25¢ for exposition attendees. (From the collection of the Parthenon, Metro Parks.)

The Gerst Alhambra was a reproduction of the famous Rathskeller beer halls in Berlin and Bremen, Germany. The building featured a large, arched beer cellar at was decorated in traditional Bavarian fashion. The beer hall also offered conventional German musical entertainment. (From the collection of the Parthenon, Metro Parks.)

The William Gerst Brewing Company's display at the Centennial Exposition was an impressive sight. The pavilion was constructed of columns made of beer bottles and had a huge cask in the back that is said to have the capacity of 2,500 gallons of beer. Demonstrations of bottling Gerst beer were performed here. Notice several of the lithographs displayed at the exhibit, which are shown earlier in this chapter. (From the collection of the Parthenon, Metro Parks.)

Once William Gerst won the gold medal at the Centennial Exposition, all of his advertising boasted this feat. One of the more popular items distributed by William Gerst was a souvenir pocket calendar. This leather-bound booklet also included such useful information as antidotes for poison and a place to enter the make of your bicycle or the size of your hat, gloves, hosiery, etc. The back reflects the large expansion to the brewery made during the past several years since the days of the old Nashville Brewery. (From the collection of Scott R. Mertie.)

NASHVILLE BREWERY.

Superior Brands of BEER.

DRAUGHT

Pilsener,—
Genuine
Lager.

BOTTLED

Pilsener Export,
Extra Pale
Bohemian.

REGISTERED.

Compliments of
William Gerst
Brewing Co.

Nashville, TENN.

This celluloid handout indicates that although it was clearly the William Gerst Brewing Company, the Nashville Brewery name was also still used. This item was handed out to attendees of the exposition prior to Gerst winning the gold medal. (From the collection of Sam Hunt.)

The two examples of etched beer glasses were used in the restaurants at the Centennial Exposition. Both glasses advertise that the William Gerst Brewing Company won the gold medal. There are eight versions of these glasses that are known to exist, although not all boasted the gold medal victory of 1897. (From the collection of Sam Hunt.)

William Gerst wanted to make sure he was able to provide advertising items to women as well as men. He had this celluloid pocket mirror made and handed out to women at the Centennial Exposition. Essentially it is a version of a modern-day compact. (From the collection of Sam Hunt.)

Diehl and Lord also had a large presence at the Tennessee Centennial Exposition. Although they were not a brewery, they bottled national brands of beer and wanted to make sure that their products were represented at the event. This advertisement was used in the exposition programs and lists all of their products, including Schlitz malt extract for nursing mothers. (From the collection of Scott R. Mertie.)

The Diehl and Lord first-class restaurant and café is shown here at the Centennial Exposition. This was direct competition with Gerst's restaurants. This building was called the Lion Roof Garden and advertises Lion Beer from Cincinnati's Widnisch-Muhllauser Brewing Company as the "finest of Earth." (From the collection of the Parthenon, Metro Parks.)

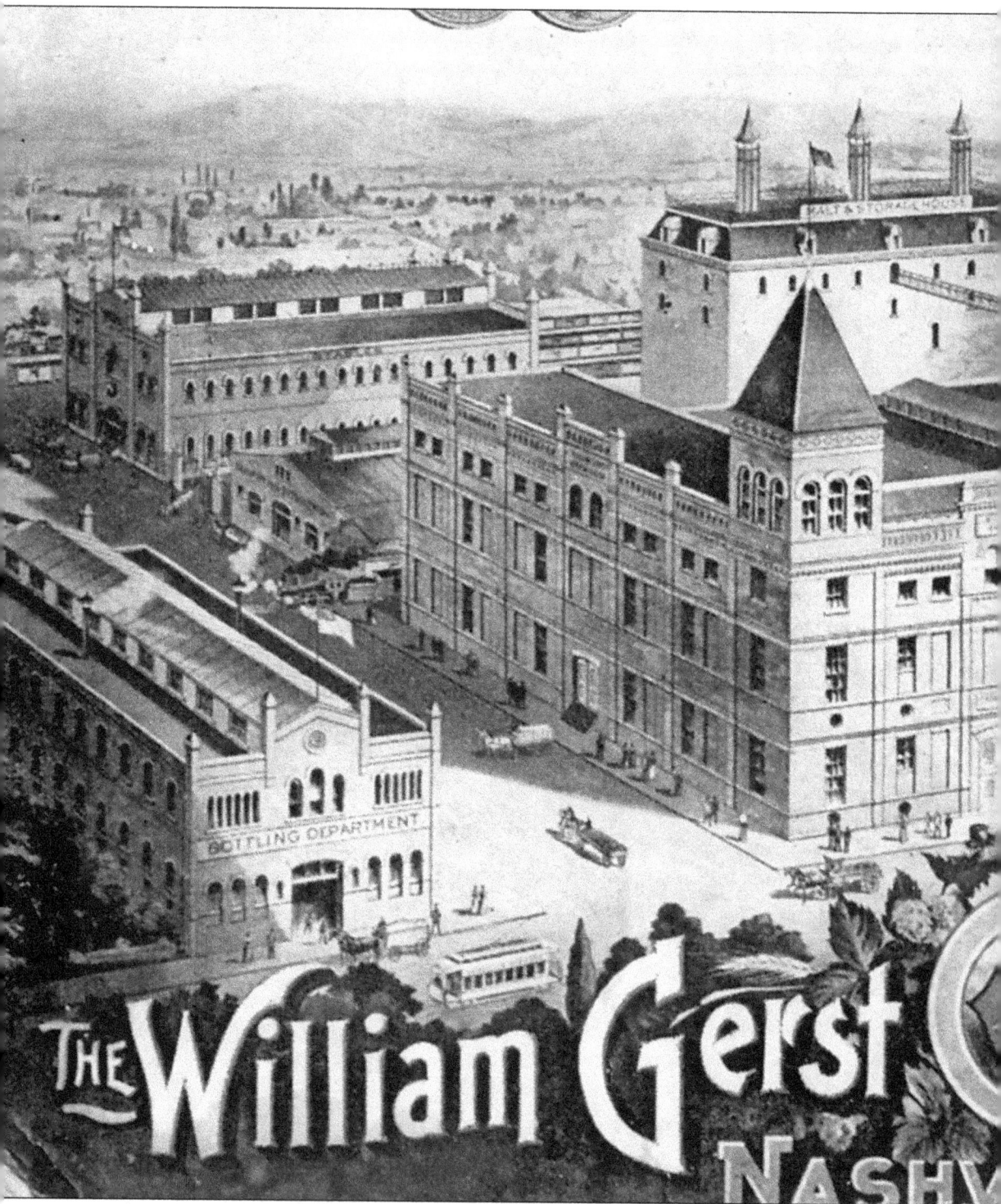

THE William Gerst
Nashv

This lithograph was made shortly after winning the gold medal at the Tennessee Centennial
Exposition. Although the brewery pictured in this lithograph is a bit exaggerated, which was
quite common in this era, the actual brewery did occupy approximately four acres. This highly

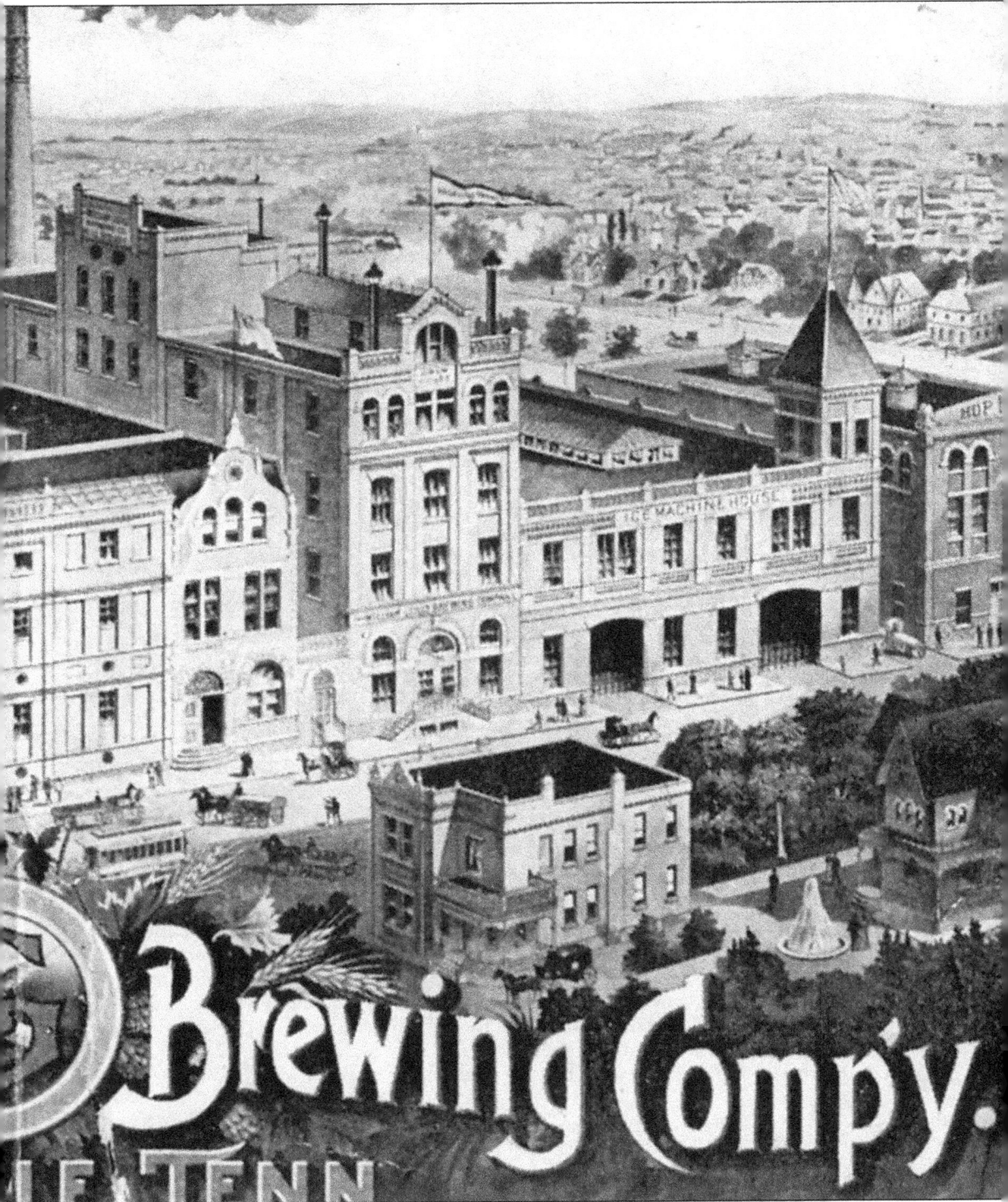

collectible lithograph was manufactured by the Milwaukee Litho and Engraving Company. It can currently be seen hanging behind the hostess stand at the Nashville Gerst Haus restaurant. (Courtesy of the Gerst Haus, Nashville, Tennessee.)

FIRST FLOOR BREW-HOUSE.   TWO 65-TON REFRIGERATING MACHINES.   SECOND FLOOR BREW-HOUSE.

These three photographs are from a publication titled Nashville in the Twentieth Century, which was issued in early 1900. The bottom photograph shows two massive 65-ton refrigeration machines that were recently installed in order produce ice. The photograph on the left reflects the pumps in the first floor of the brew house that would pump beer to the other six levels in the brewery. The photograph on the right shows the tops of the copper brew kettles on the second floor of the brew house. During this time, the brewery had an annual capacity of 40,000 to 50,000 barrels. (Courtesy of the Nashville Room, Tennessee Public Library.)

Pictured are several extremely rare samples of early pre-prohibition beer labels. Pilsener was Gerst's most popular brand, and it was brewed for many years to come. Maritana was another short-lived brand brewed by Gerst. Note that both labels indicate that the brewery has its own bottling plant. Prior to mass-production bottling lines, beer labels were die-cut and applied to each bottle by hand. Once the automated bottling line was adopted, the standard rectangular label was applied by machine. The Milwaukee Lithograph Company printed these two examples for Gerst. (From the collection of Scott R. Mertie.)

This lithograph from 1898 shows a number of children playing in a William Gerst Brewing Company Wagon. At this time, it was common for beer and other alcohol advertising to include children. (From the collection of Herb and Helen Haydock.)

This lithograph from 1899 shows an unknown woman sitting on a daybed with a William Gerst Brewing Company pillow. The print almost looks like a valentine, as it is accented in a beaded and lace pink boarder. (From the collection of Scott R. Mertie.)

Crystal Beer was another short-lived brand brewed by Gerst around 1900. Other than this beer label, no other advertising is known to exist for Gerst's Crystal Beer. (From the collection of Scott R. Mertie.)

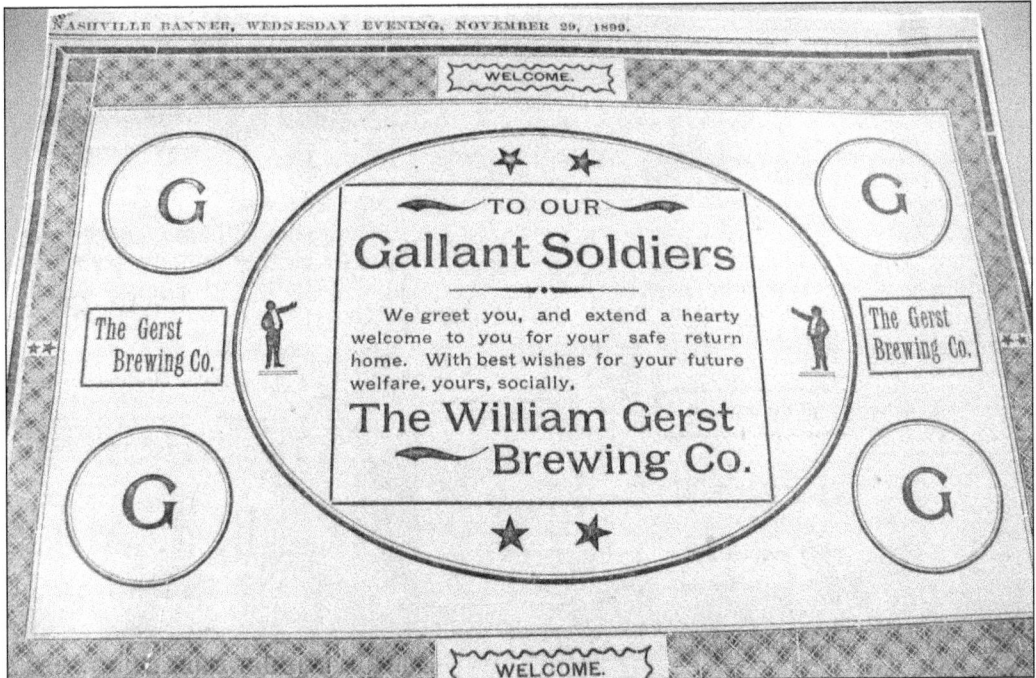

This advertisement in the November 29, 1899, *Nashville Banner* was placed by Gerst to welcome home America's gallant soldiers from the Spanish-American War. (From the collection of Terry Williams.)

This photograph is believed to be taken inside the tap room at the William Gerst Brewing Company. The bar is fully stocked and includes some highly collectible Jack Daniel's bottles. The lithograph hanging on the wall was issued by the brewery in the early 1900s. Although difficult to see in this picture, a Gerst Brewery sign is also hanging above the bar. (From the collection of the Tennessee State Library and Archives.)

This beautiful lithograph that was hanging at the taproom in the brewery can now bee seen at Gerst Haus restaurants in Nashville and Evansville. Several other examples are known to exist in personal collections. The original piece was painted by the noted artist Asti, whose works of art were used by many breweries and other European companies. The model is wearing a gown, which is an extremely vibrant red color. (From the collection of the Gerst Haus, Nashville, Tennessee.)

Another lithograph was issued to complement the previous piece, only this one is accented with brilliant green coloring. It can also be seen at both Gerst Haus restaurants. Most of the lithographs advertising during this time period did not bother including information about the brewery or their beers. It simply showed a nice painting with the brewery's name written above or below it. (From the collection of the Gerst Haus, Nashville, Tennessee.)

Breweries often issued calendars to saloons and other business owners as another form of advertising. Often the calendar would hang in the establishment the entire year. This calendar from 1904 had "tear off" pages for each month. (From the collection of Norman Jay.)

The William Gerst Brewing Company issued a number of corncob pipes around the beginning of the 20th century. Several variations are known to exist. Notice the long stem, which is approximately 18 inches long. (From the collection of Scott R. Mertie.)

The first beer tray known to be issued by the William Gerst Brewing Company is commonly known as the "Centennial Tray," as it reflects Gerst winning the gold medal at the 1897 Centennial Exposition. This is a highly collectible piece of breweriana. (From the collection of Norman Jay.)

This beer tray from 1910 is a fine example of a "Gibson Girl." The tray advertises "Gerst's Bottled Beer for Family Use." It was once rumored that the girl shown on this tray was one of Gerst's two daughters, but that was later disbanded as the same model was found on some other brewery advertising pieces in Canada. The "Gibson Girl" was a name given for a style of female model made popular by illustrator Charles Dana Gibson in the early 20th century. (From the collection of Norman Jay.)

The William Gerst Brewing Company issued four wildlife lithographs in 1907. These colorful lithographs were printed in Germany under contract by Raphael Tuck and Sons of New York. These four lithographs hang in the Nashville Gerst Haus and in some personal collections today.

The four lithographs are titled as follows: *Pheasants* (from the collection of Scott R. Mertie); *Partridges* (from the collection of Scott R. Mertie); *Mallards* (from the collection of the Gerst Haus, Nashville, Tennessee); and *Brook Trout* (from the collection of Sam Hunt.)

The William Gerst Brewing Company adopted the dove brand as a way to enlighten the public of the purity of Gerst Beer. Early beers brewed under this brand where Bohemian style and pale export beer. These labels boast that the brewery had its own bottling line, which was a status symbol of the day among breweries, especially over the brands that were shipped to Diehl and Lord to be bottled at their distributing warehouse. (From the collection of Scott R. Mertie.)

Although some beer was bottled, most of the beer distributed by the William Gerst Brewing Company in the early 1900s was in still in casks. This picture shows brewery workers kegging Gerst beer to be distributed to area saloons and taverns. (From the collection of the Nashville Room, Tennessee Public Library.)

This same style cask is pictured here as it was in the picture above. Two sizes of these wooden casks were used at saloons to dispense their draft Gerst beer. A wood crate is also shown that was used to transport 24 bottles. (From the collection of Scott R. Mertie.)

WM. GERST
Proprietor the Wm. Gerst Brewing Co.
Nashville

This sketch was printed in a book called *Tennesseans as We See Them*. The sketch shows William Gerst sitting on a wood beer crate reading *The Horseman* and *How to Bread Race Horses*. His stables and brewery are shown in the background. (From the collection of the Nashville Room, Tennessee Public Library.)

William Gerst's home, Vine Hill, was a magnificent mansion located near the brewery. Unfortunately, the home was destroyed decades ago to make room for government housing. This rare photograph of Vine Hill appeared in *Pen and Sunlight Sketches of Nashville*. (From the collection of the Nashville Room, Tennessee Public Library.)

Donau
1910

When not focused on his brewery, William Gerst was involved with his second passion—horse racing. Gerst maintained stables in South Nashville and had raced several horses at the Kentucky Derby in the early 1900s. Finally, in 1910, his horse by the name of Donau won the Kentucky Derby in 2 minutes and 6.5 seconds. An announcer at the Kentucky Derby described Donau having "the speed of a sprinter, the courage of a bulldog, and the gaminess of a fighting cock." (From the collection of Scott R. Mertie.)

Donau is the German name for the Danube River, which was located near Gerst's hometown in Germany. This painting hung over William Gerst's desk in his office at the brewery. The same painting is currently displayed at the Gerst Haus in Nashville. Robert Herbert was the jockey that road Donau into the winner's circle at the 36th annual Kentucky Derby. (From the collection of the Gerst Haus, Nashville Tennessee.)

William Gerst retired from his brewing business after the implementation of Prohibition. He left the brewery and bottling works to be run by his four sons and retired to Cincinnati. Gerst died on March 10, 1933, and never got to see his brewery after the repeal of Prohibition that same year. (From the collection of Jack Gerst.)

Gerst was buried at the Spring Grove Cemetery in Cincinnati, along with other prominent brewers. His wife, Margaret, died five years later on February 2, 1938, and is buried beside him. (Photograph taken by Phil Nuxhall, historian and tour coordinator for the Heritage Foundation of Spring Grove Cemetery and Arboretum.)

William Gerst's headstone has his family's coat of arms engraved in the granite. (Photograph taken by Phil Nuxhall, historian and tour coordinator for the Heritage Foundation of Spring Grove Cemetery and Arboretum.)

The family Gerst descends from the very ancient, formerly noble generation of the Gersts of Castle Gerst in Tyrol (Austria), which in the 16th century settled in Suabia (Wurttenberg in Southern Germany), where they also used the surname von Raverstain. In 1544, however, the original family died out in the male line. The coat of arms is composed of a shield divided into four sections with a blue background; there are two crossed ears of barley (Gerst) which, on a triple peaked mountain, represents the name and generation; in a silver field, a red cross beam signifies prominence; six lilies indicate high virtue. The open, crowned helmet symbolizes noble ancestry. The jewel in the helmet testifies upsurge and respect for the noble virtues. The shield is being kept in the collection of shields of F. Lerch in Munich. (From the collection Jack Gerst.)

This photograph is of two of William Gerst's grandchildren, August and Elizabeth, riding in their buggy at Vine Hill. August (junior) and Elizabeth are the children of August Gerst (senior, son of William Gerst) and Elizabeth Schneider. Unfortunately, August Gerst (junior) was killed by his father-in-law in 1940 during a family feud. (From the collection Patricia Gerst Benson.)

This photograph is of August L. Gerst Sr. at the family's camp on the Harpeth River. August learned to brew from his father and eventually assumed the duties of brewmaster and later president of the brewery as his father eased into retirement. The brewery continued to operate as a family business. In addition to August, William's other sons worked at the brewery: George served as vice president, Albert as secretary and bottling superintendent, and William J. as advertising manager. (From the collection Patricia Gerst Benson.)

Three

THOSE HORRIBLE YEARS OF PROHIBITION

At the beginning of the century, the Temperance Movement was in full gear pushing for national prohibition. This advertisement reflecting Teddy Roosevelt shooting a bear was in the October 27, 1907, *Tennessean* newspaper. The Gerst Brewery is advertising in this advertisement that their beer is "mild," in hopes of appeasing those pushing for prohibition. (From the collection of the Gerst Haus, Nashville, Tennessee.)

In an effort to increase sales by promoting nonalcoholic beverages, the Gerst Bottling Works was started to produce colas, seltzers, and other malt beverages. (From the collection of Scott R. Mertie.)

Gerst Select was a cereal beverage or "near beer" produced by the William Gerst Brewing Company during Prohibition. Select contained less than "1/2 of 1%" of alcohol by volume. (From the collection of Scott R. Mertie.)

These two ads were placed in the Nashville *Tennessean* newspaper in 1922 promoting Gerst Select. The top advertisement also reminds readers not to forget their Orange, Lemon, and Lime Crushes as well as newly introduced Delaware Punch. (From the collection of Scott R. Mertie.)

THE WILLIAM GERST BREWING CO.

AND

GERST BOTTLINC WORKS

NASHVILLE, TENN.

THE PERFECT TEMPERANCE DRINK
SELECT
MADE TO CONTAIN ½ OF 1 PER CENT. OF ALCOHOL

This receipt was issued on June 24, 1918, for Gerst Select. It is interesting to note the receipt reflects Select as the "perfect temperance drink." The receipt is also stamped to "please return empties promptly." (From the collection of Scott R. Mertie.)

One lithograph issued under the Gerst Bottling Works name is known to exist. Since taverns were closed during this time period, most brewery advertising ceased to exist. In fact, many lithographs had the brewery reference painted over and the pieces were displayed in people's homes. (From the collection of Norman Jay.)

The Gerst Bottling Works dealt largely with carbonated waters and issued seltzer and soda water to restaurants in etched bottles like the one shown here. This bottle has a stainless pressure valve at the top, which is engraved "Gerst Seltzer Water." (From the collection of Terry Williams.)

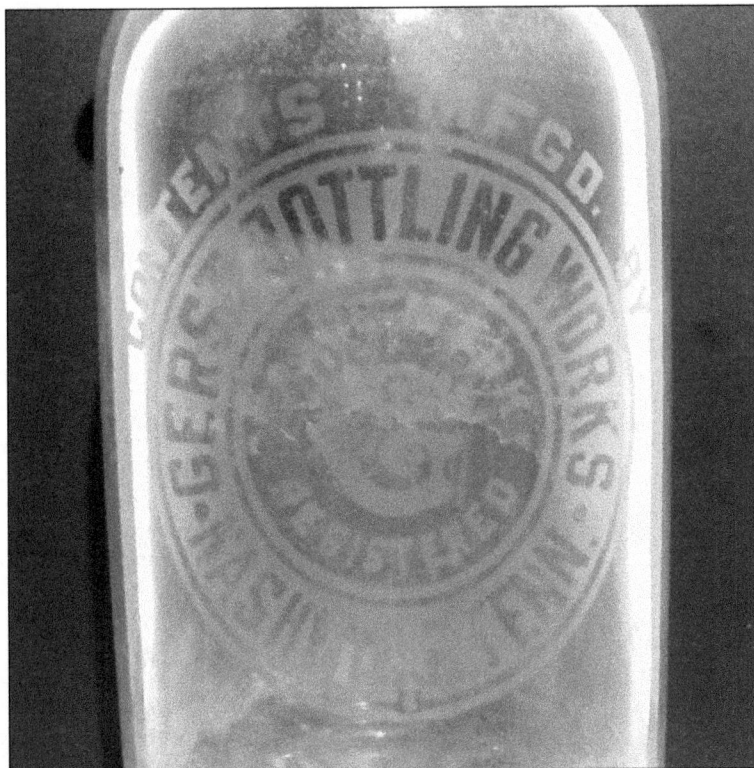

SUPERIOR PRODUCTS
"Since 1890"

GERST PILSNER BEER
AND
GERST OLD STYLE ALE

CARBONATED BEVERAGES
ORANGE CRUSH
NATURAL SET UP
HI-LIFE WATER
CLEO COLA
DELAWARE PUNCH
GINGER ALE

Gerst Sodas - In the Distinctive
12 Oz. Bottles - All Flavors

The Wm. Gerst Brewing Co., Inc.
NASHVILLE, TENN.   PHONE 6-1893

"What Tennessee Makes -
Makes Tennessee"

ATLANTA SALESBOOK CO., ATLANTA, GA. 79△656

After the repeal of Prohibition in 1933, the Gerst Bottling Works continued to manufacture and distribute various colas and other carbonated beverages, including Orange Crush. This is the back of a 1940 receipt and lists the entire line of nonalcoholic beverages produced by the Gerst Bottling Works. (From the collection of Scott R. Mertie.)

These painted-label bottles are from the Gerst Bottling Works and are from around 1940. The bottle on the left is Gerst Sparkling Beverage, and on the right is an Orange Crush bottle. The back of the Sparkling Beverage bottle reads "Gerst: For quality, for taste, for satisfaction. Made from the finest flavors and pure cane sugar." The back of the amber Orange Crush bottle reads "This special bottle protects the delicate fruit flavor and fresh taste." (From the collection of Scott R. Mertie.)

This Orange Crush advertisement was placed by Gerst along with about 20 other companies and distributed on a colorful Nashville city fan. The fan is made of cardboard and attached to a stick to help cool one's self from the hot and humid Nashville heat. (From the collection of Scott R. Mertie.)

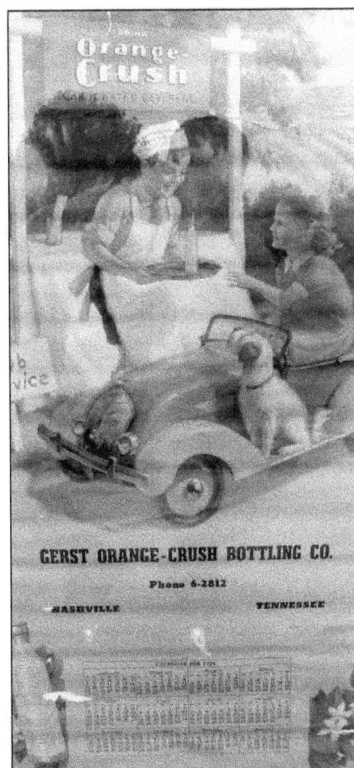

This 1938–1939 Orange Crush calendar was issued by the Gerst Orange Crush Bottling Works. Although difficult to appreciate in this photograph, the calendar is very colorful and detailed. (From the collection of Sam Hunt.)

The Gerst Bottling Works tried to compete in the cola business, but such brands as Pepsi and Coca-Cola had cornered the market. Gerst bottled Vess Cola for a brief period in the 1940s, but decided to stick to crushes and sparkling waters. (From the collection of Norman Jay.)

With the adoption of the crown bottle cap, breweries often gave away church keys, or bottle openers, to consumers in order for them to open the beverages. Of course this became another form of advertising for breweries. This opener is from the 1940s and is engraved, "Gerst's sodas are best" on the front and "Try our cola" on the back. (From the collection of Scott R. Mertie.)

Four

THE RETURN OF BEER
IN NASHVILLE

"The business will begin manufacturing, brewing, bottling, and selling beer of an alcoholic content as nor or hereafter made legal under the federal statutes and the statutes of the State of Tennessee." This was the wording of the Amendment to the Charter of Incorporation for the William Gerst Brewing Company on April 26, 1933. Prohibition has been repealed and breweries all over the county began operating again. Production began immediately once the William Gerst Brewing Company's amendment to the corporate charter was approved by the state. (From the collection of the Tennessee State Library and Archives.)

These two photographs show the impressive brew house and enormous hop house used by the William Gerst Brewing Company. These structures were designed by the L. Schreiber and Son's Company and were impressive landmarks in Nashville until the brewery was demolished in 1963. (From the collection of the Tennessee State Library and Archives.)

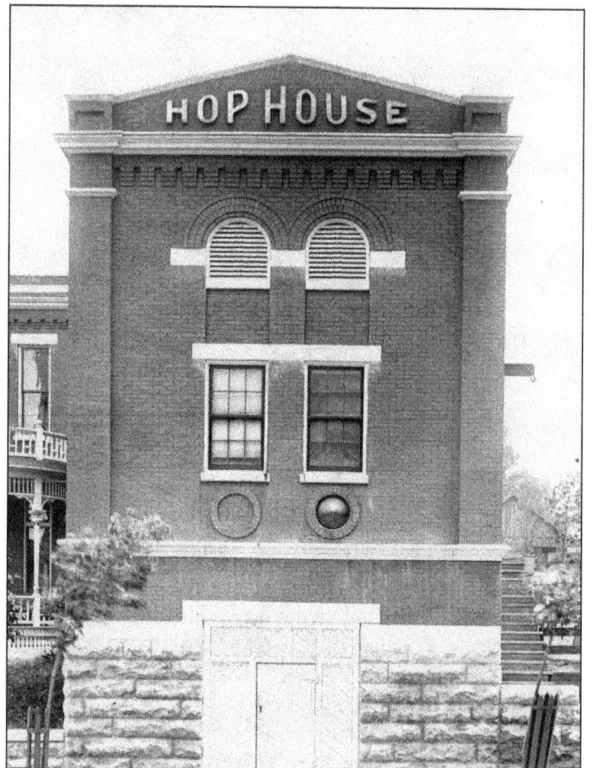

Gerst's Gold Medal '97 Beer Makes Debut At Tenn. State Fair

In 1934, the William Gerst Brewing Company installed a new bottling line that was able to fill 120 bottles of beer a minute. This new bottling machine contained foamless bottle fillers which increased sanitary conditions and eliminated cracked or nicked bottles, insuring a better product for consumers. This story in the Nashville *Tennessean* shows a rare picture of the bottling line and also tells of Gerst reintroducing its famous recipe that won the gold medal in 1897. (From the collection of the Nashville Room, Tennessee Public Library.)

These crowns (bottle caps) reflect a variety of brands brewed and distributed by the William Gerst Brewing Company after the repeal of Prohibition. These would have been capped on bottles using the new bottling line shown in the newspaper article above. (From the collection of Scott R. Mertie.)

The William Gerst Brewing Company was the first brewery to register in the State of Tennessee after the repeal of Prohibition in 1933. Breweries were required to display their federal U-type permit number as well as indicate that federal tax had been paid. Gerst Pale Beer and Dark Beer were some of the first beers brewed after Prohibition. These two labels are very early examples of this new law; "tax paid at the rate prescribed by the Internal Revenue Law" and "does not contain more than 4% alcohol by volume" are clearly displayed on the label. (From the collection of Scott R. Mertie.)

By 1935, new beer labeling regulations were passed and the alcohol restrictions did not have to be printed. Also, the fancy wording about the tax was limited to "Internal Revenue Tax Paid," or "IRTP." By this time, the Dove Brand trademark was no longer used, but the brewery included its new slogan, "Brewed in Dixie". (From the collection of Scott R. Mertie.)

OLD ORIGINAL
Gerst
BEER
·· BREWED IN DIXIE ··

In an effort to recruit pre-prohibition drinkers back to Gerst, the brewery advertised its brand as "Old Original Beer." This third rendition of a Gerst beer tray also includes the popular "Brewed in Dixie" slogan. (From the collection of Scott R. Mertie.)

Once the early post-prohibition alcohol restrictions were lifted, Gerst began advertising its Old Original as having up to 6.25 percent alcohol by volume. This neck label was used on Gerst's Old Style Ale bottles in the late 1930s. (From the collection of Scott R. Mertie.)

By 1937, Gerst started brewing Old Lager, which was advertised as being "made and aged the old fashioned way." This brand was believed to be brewed from the same recipe as Old Jug Lager was 47 years earlier. By the late 1930s, the U-permit number was no longer required to be printed on labels. (From the collection of Scott R. Mertie.)

Gerst Pilsner Beer was also introduced in the late 1930s and was very popular well into the 1940s. This advertisement states that Gerst Pilsner Beer is "Always in Good Taste—Always Tastes Good." (From the collection of Scott R. Mertie.)

In 1940, the William Gerst Brewing Company reached 50 years of continuous operations. To celebrate its 50th anniversary, the brewery started a large advertising campaign. Large, two-color ads were placed in newspapers thanking Nashville customers for their loyal patronage over the years. Although William Gerst passed away seven years earlier, his sons still used his picture on the advertisement. (From the collection of Scott R. Mertie.)

The advertising campaign lasted the entire season and used the Gay Nineties as its theme. The real spectacle of the campaign was presented to the people of Nashville when a couple dressed in Victorian clothing rode through the streets in a horse and buggy. Pictures were published in newspapers as well as in this 50th-anniversary postcard. (From the collection of Scott R. Mertie.)

Ads were printed in a variety of newspapers in the South indicating the 50th anniversary of the William Gerst Brewing Company. The slogan "with those who thirst the word is Gerst" was used commonly on advertisements. (From the collection of Scott R. Mertie.)

This Gerst Pilsner Label still reflects the Internal Revue Tax Paid statement and boasts that it is made using the "Choicest Materials" and is made from "All Grain." This label can be seen on many of the advertisements on the preceding pages. (From the collection of Scott R. Mertie.)

Cardboard signs were used in the early 1940s, as metal became scarce due to World War II. The top self-framed sign is depicting life 50 years earlier as two couples prepare for a picnic on their wagon with a keg of Gerst beer. The cardboard sign below was used to market to the outdoorsman by showing Gerst Pilsner along with fly-fishing equipment. (Top from the collection of Scott R. Mertie; bottom from the collection of Norman Jay.)

The William Gerst Brewing Company did not issue many neon signs. The Old Original neon sign shown here is currently hanging at the Gerst Haus restaurant in Evansville. (From the collection of the Gerst Haus, Evansville, Indiana.)

The William Gerst Brewing Company issued several types of porcelain signs in the 1940s. This example is three feet tall by two feet wide and boasts the "Brewed in Dixie" slogan. (From the collection of Sam Hunt.)

Both of these porcelain signs were also issued by the William Gerst Brewing Company in the 1940s. The one pictured above is more prevalent than the one shown below. Both are approximately three feet wide by two feet tall and have a bright red background. (From the collection of Sam Hunt.)

A series of photographs printed on cardboard were used as advertisements for Gerst Pilsner Beer during the 1940s. The first one shown here is titled *Pals* and shows a man enjoying a Gerst Pilsner Beer with his German shepherd. The second photograph is titled *For Pleasure* and captures two couples enjoying a picnic lunch with the same German shepherd and of course, Gerst Pilsner. (Top from the collection of the Gerst Haus, Nashville, Tennessee; bottom from the collection of Sam Hunt.)

ALWAYS IN GOOD TASTE

Your friends will appreciate your Good Taste if, next time, you serve Gerst Pilsner. We who make this magnificent beer naturally think it the grandest ever bottled. Nor is it hard to understand, once you've tasted Gerst Pilsner, why so many others share our enthusiasm. In short, we venture to say that if you are not among those who consider Gerst Pilsner one of the finest beers in America, it's simply because you haven't tried it. In that case . . . won't you? The William Gerst Brewing Co., Inc. Nashville, Tenn.

Gerst
PILSNER BEER
ALWAYS IN GOOD TASTE · ALWAYS TASTES GOOD

BUY MORE WAR BONDS AND KEEP THEM

When America entered World War II, it was common for breweries to promote the war effort and support the America troops. This Gerst Pilsner "always in good taste" advertisement appeared in the June 6, 1944, version of the Nashville *Tennessean*. The cover story of the paper is about the U.S. troops landing at Normandy, France. At the bottom, the advertisement states, "Buy more war bonds and keep them." (From the collection of Scott R. Mertie.)

Advertising for war bonds became so popular that the William Gerst Brewing Company even started placing them on their neck labels. This "Buy War Bonds" neck label is from a Gerst Old Style Ale bottle. (From the collection of Scott R. Mertie.)

AMERICA'S LINE OF "THIRST" DEFENSE

As America became more patriotic during World War II, so did the brewery advertising. These two, self-framed cardboard advertisements for Gerst Pilsner Beer reflect the brewery's support for the American troops. The first sign advertises Gerst is "America's Line of 'Thirst' Defense," while the second says "America's Thirst Calls for Gerst Pilsner Beer." Both of these ads were produced with vibrant colors. (From the collection of Scott R. Mertie.)

By 1947, the William Gerst Brewing Company had been producing beer for 57 years. William J. Gerst and August L. Gerst decided to promote their flagship pilsner beer as Gerst 57 Pilsner Beer. This brand continued for the next seven years until the brewery closed in 1954. The brewery issued many promotional items advertising Gerst 57, including the beer glass and tin sign shown here. (From the collection of Scott R. Mertie.)

Small tab knobs were much more popular in the early years over the taller tap handles because they didn't take up nearly as much space. The William Gerst Brewing Company issued two ball tap knobs during its existence. Pictured here is the rarer of the two, which is for Gerst 57. (From the collection of Scott R. Mertie.)

Up until the late 1940s, most beer bottles were able to be returned for a refund. Several glass companies started marketing a thinner bottle that was considered to be disposable. Salesmen would make samples of a prospective brewery's popular brands and call on the brewery to convince them to switch from the traditional heavy returnable bottles. Here are the only two known examples of Gerst mini-bottles pictured with an actual Gerst 57 Pilsner Beer "no deposit—no return"–embossed bottle. (From the collection of Scott R. Mertie.)

Many reverse-painted glasses were used by breweries to advertise their beers in bar windows during the 1940s and 1950s. This Gerst 57 Premium Beer reverse-painted glass is a common collectible issued by the brewery. (From the collection of Scott R. Mertie.)

Beer salesmen often wore buttons on their jackets promoting the beers they were pushing. Pictured here are an Old Original "Brewed in Dixie" Beer button from the late 1930s and a Gerst 57 Beer button from the late 1940s. (From the collection of Scott R. Mertie.)

The Labelgram Company of Detroit, Michigan, came up with an idea to print trivia questions on the back of beer labels. The labels were designed with a perforated middle section that was not glued to the bottle and could be easily torn off. The William Gerst Brewing Company purchased several variations of these Labelgram labels for use on their products in the late 1940s. (From the collection of Scott R. Mertie.)

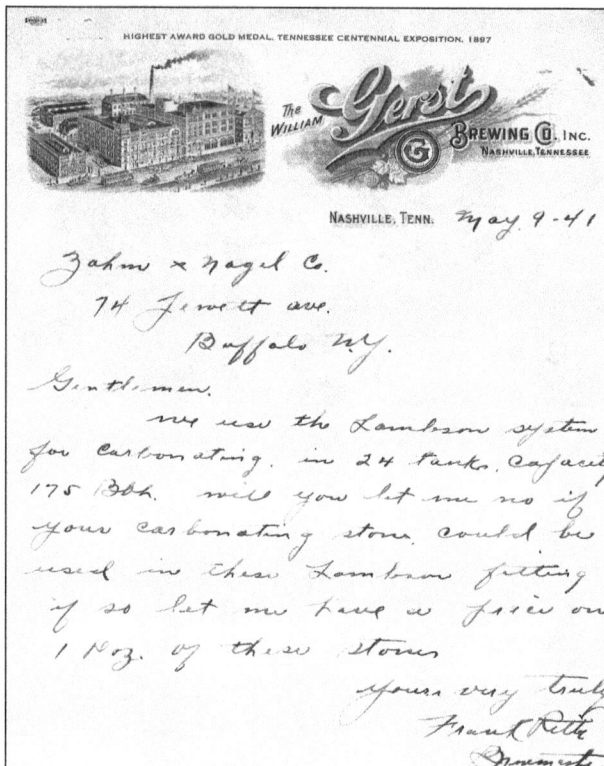

It was common for companies to print elaborate sketches of their breweries on their letterhead and envelopes. Here are two versions of letterhead from 1941 and 1947, respectively. The second letter was written by William J. Gerst to the Tennessee Brewing Company in Memphis, Tennessee. (From the collection of Scott R. Mertie.)

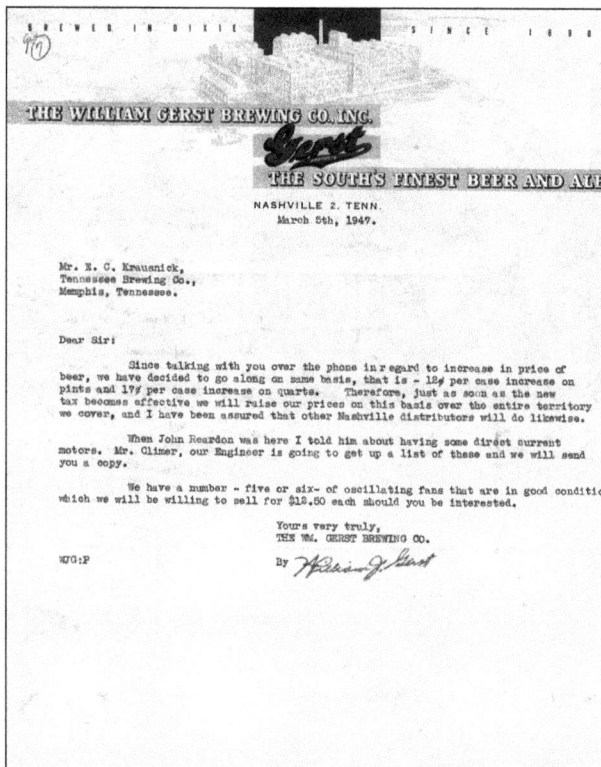

By the late 1940s, national breweries were making it difficult to compete for smaller regional breweries. Many developed new brands of beer to try and catch the eye of the consumer. The William Gerst Brewing Company developed a new all-grain beer called Kings Oasis, or K-O Ale for short. Two versions of the K-O label were produced during its short lifespan. This first image is a tin sign with one version of the label. Below is a label showing the second version of the artwork. (From the collection of Scott R. Mertie.)

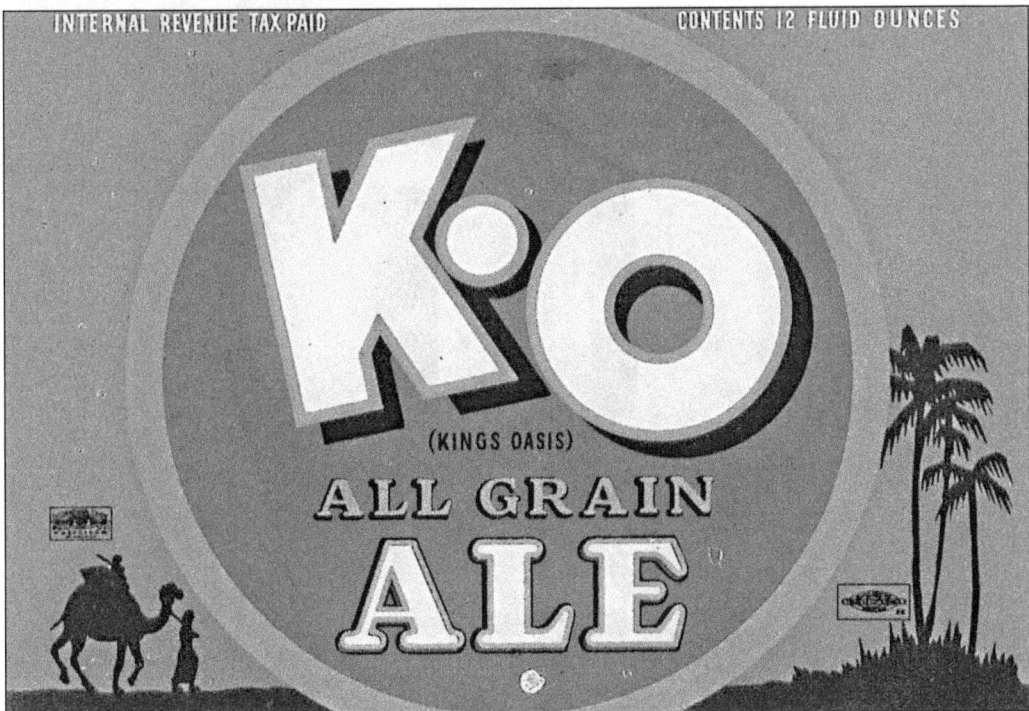

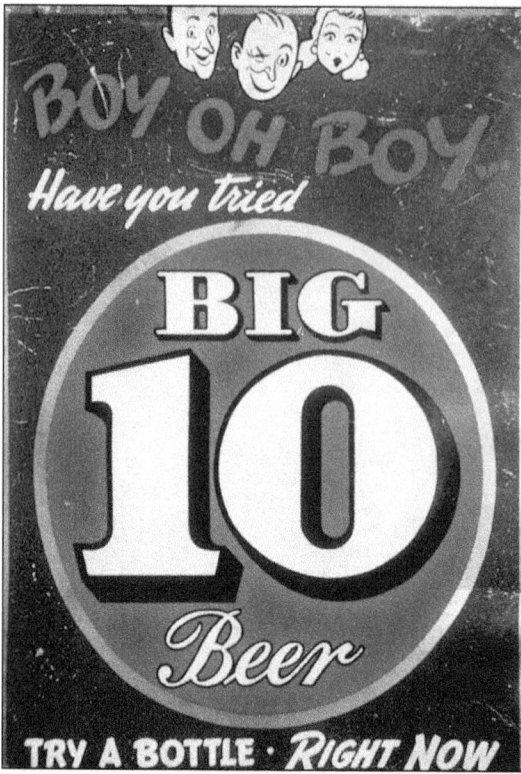

Big 10 Beer was another new brand that the William Gerst Brewing Company introduced in the late 1940s. This advertisement is printed on a cardboard sign with a cute cartoon image asking customers if they have tried Big 10 Beer. (From the collection of Norman Jay.)

Gerst marketed the Big 10 Beer brand across all of Tennessee. The graphic on the label showed the entire state. (From the collection of Scott R. Mertie.)

The William Gerst Brewing Company advertised its brands all over Tennessee. This picture shows a car in the garage at a Hillsboro Village filling station. The tire cover on the back of the vehicle advertises Gerst Beer and has the familiar quote, "Brewed in Dixie." (From the collection of Scott R. Mertie.)

Elaborate beer displays were designed to catch the attention of shoppers in area grocery stores. This display in a Nashville market is for Pabst Blue Ribbon Beer and Pabst Blue Ribbon Ale. Pabst was one of the national brands that took the market share away from Gerst. (From the collection of Scott R. Mertie.)

Prior to Interstate 40, travelers had to take Highway 70 to get from Nashville to Memphis. This picture was taken at the Highways 70 and 100 split. Behind the "turn right to Memphis" sign, a billboard can be seen with the words "Drink Gerst Beer" on it. Ironically a Schlitz Beer billboard is right next to it. (From the collection of Scott R. Mertie.)

By the end of the 1940s, the Gerst family was having a difficult time operating the brewery in a financially sound manner. It was decided to sell the brewery in 1950. A group of Nashville investors purchased the brewery for a reported $400,000. The new owners kept the Gerst name and William J. Gerst continued to work for the new owners. The new Gerst brewery continued to brew some of the same brands, but introduced a new brand called Brew 77 later that year. (From the collection of the Nashville Room, Tennessee Public Library.)

Back bar displays were commonly used by breweries in the 1940s and 1950s to market brands to a potential consumer sitting on a bar stool. Most were made of chalk and were simple cartoon characters or brewery logos. A series of chalk displays were made in Louisville that had a hand reaching up holding a can or bottle of beer. This is the only known version of a Gerst chalk display advertising the Gerst Brew 77. (From the collection of Norman Jay.)

The two most popular brands brewed by the William Gerst Brewing Company in the 1950s were Gerst 57 Premium Beer and Gerst Brew 77 Extra Dry beer. The Gerst 57 bottle reflects a change to the label; most notably, the IRTP (Internal Revenue Tax Paid) stamp was no longer required.

The new owners of the brewery invested in a canning line, and for several years, Gerst 57 was available in a crowntainer and Brew 77 was available in a conetop. Both cans were produced by two different can manufacturers and are highly sought after by beer can collectors. (From the collection of Scott R. Mertie.)

By 1952, competition was making it difficult for the new owners of the William Gerst Brewing Company to continue operating the facility. One last attempt was made at introducing several new brands into the market. Gerst Old Amber Premium Beer was an Oktoberfest-style beer that varied from the traditional light pilsners that had been produced for so many years. The brewery also introduced Ten-E-Cee Hom-Bru in 1953. This was marketed only to Tennesseans and it simply stated that it "is good beer." These were the last brands ever produced by the brewery. (From the collection of Scott R. Mertie.)

This is one of the last photographs of the William Gerst Brewing Company taken as an operating brewery. A large billboard advertising Gerst's Brew 77 Beer was painted on the side of the brewery for all of South Nashville to see. (From the collection of Scott Mertie.)

The William Gerst Brewing Company officially ceased all brewing production in the last week of February 1954. This photograph shows former brewery workers enjoying a keg of Gerst Beer in March 1954, several weeks after the brewery closed. The keg was purchased by S. L. Wade (center) for $7.01. (From the collection of the Nashville and Davidson County Archives.)

The former William Gerst Brewing Company stood vacant for the next few years until it was purchased by a Memphis company in 1957. The brewery was stripped of its equipment and sold for scrap, while the rest of the facility was used as warehouse space. (From the collection of the Nashville Room, Tennessee Public Library.)

The main brewhouse was demolished on May 17, 1963, by the Burke Wrecking Company. A warehouse was built at the brewery's former location on Sixth Avenue South. The building that housed the bottling line still stood at 800 Ewing Avenue and was used as a warehouse by the Breeding Insulation Company until it burned down in the early morning hours of April 26, 1992. (From the collection of the Nashville Room, Tennessee Public Library.)

Five

THE GERST NAME CONTINUES

In 1955, William J. Gerst, grandson of William Gerst, opened the Gerst Haus restaurant in downtown Nashville at 315 Second Avenue North. Many of the items that were located in the taproom at the brewery were transported to the restaurant. These include lithographs shown earlier in this book and the painting of Donau, which hung behind William Gerst's desk in his office. (From the collection of the Nashville Room, Tennessee Public Library.)

William J. Gerst (left) is pictured inside the first Gerst Haus restaurant shortly after it opened. Although Gerst always wore a bow tie while running the restaurant, at this time, the staff did as well. Since the Gerst brewery had closed, the options for draft beer were Budweiser and Oertle's 92. Signs for Braumeister and Thuringer sandwiches hang behind the bar. Schlitz, Carling's Black Label, and Oertle's 92 signs can be seen hanging above the bar. (From the collection of the Gerst Haus, Nashville, Tennessee.)

GERST HOUSE
GERMAN FOODS - DRAFT BEERS
*The House of Unusual Foods
at Reasonable Prices*

Near The Court House
315 — Second Ave., No.
Nashville, Tenn.

WILLIAM J. GERST, Prop.

Above is William J. Gerst's business card. It notes on the card that the Gerst House is located near the courthouse. Because of its proximity, it became the popular hangout for attorneys and politicians throughout the 1960s. Gerst's card also advertises that the Gerst House is "the house for unusual foods at reasonable prices." That is proven by the card below, which indicates a Gerst Chicken Burger can be purchased for 15¢ with the coupon. The spelling of the restaurant was later changed to the Gerst Haus in order to promote the German theme. (From the collection of Sam Hunt.)

15c

NEW - NEW

TRY IT 2⁰⁰

15c

NEW - NEW

Gerst
CHICKEN BURGER
30c
THIS CARD AND 15c (PLUS TAX) WILL BUY YOU
AN ALL NEW CHICKEN - BURGER AT
GERST HOUSE
315 SECOND AVE., N.
GOOD FOR ONLY 30 DAYS - VOID AFTER _____

15c

15c

This photograph was taken around 1960 and shows William J. Gerst and his longtime bartender, Eddie, holding up bottles of Ballantine Ale. Flat-top cases of Schlitz, Champaign Velvet, Falstaff, and Oertle's 92 beer cans can be seen sitting on the back of the bar. The back bar signage includes Carling's Black Label, Country Club Malt Liquor, Miller, and Budweiser. (From the collection of Sam Hunt.)

This photograph shows employees behind the bar at the Gerst Haus in the mid-1960s. The person on the left was nicknamed "Shorty" for obvious reasons. He worked here and at the subsequent Gerst Haus restaurants in Nashville for approximately 40 years. Notice the photograph of the Gerst's 50th Anniversary Celebration above Shorty. (From the collection of the Gerst Haus, Nashville, Tennessee.)

The menu at the Gerst Haus was hung on the wall over the kitchen. This became a tradition and was shown above the kitchen at the subsequent Gerst Haus restaurants as well. The waitress sitting at the counter on the right is Helen Woodard. She worked at the original Gerst Haus for 16 years. Coincidently her granddaughter currently works at the third incarnation of the Gerst Haus in Nashville. (From the collection of Sam Hunt.)

In addition to the main menu hanging on the wall, there were many painted cardboard signs with specials. This particular sign was for a fish sandwich with slaw for 50¢. The prices were commonly painted over to account for price increases. This framed piece also has a Gerst Haus patch with it, which was worn on employee uniforms in the early days. (From the collection of Scott R. Mertie.)

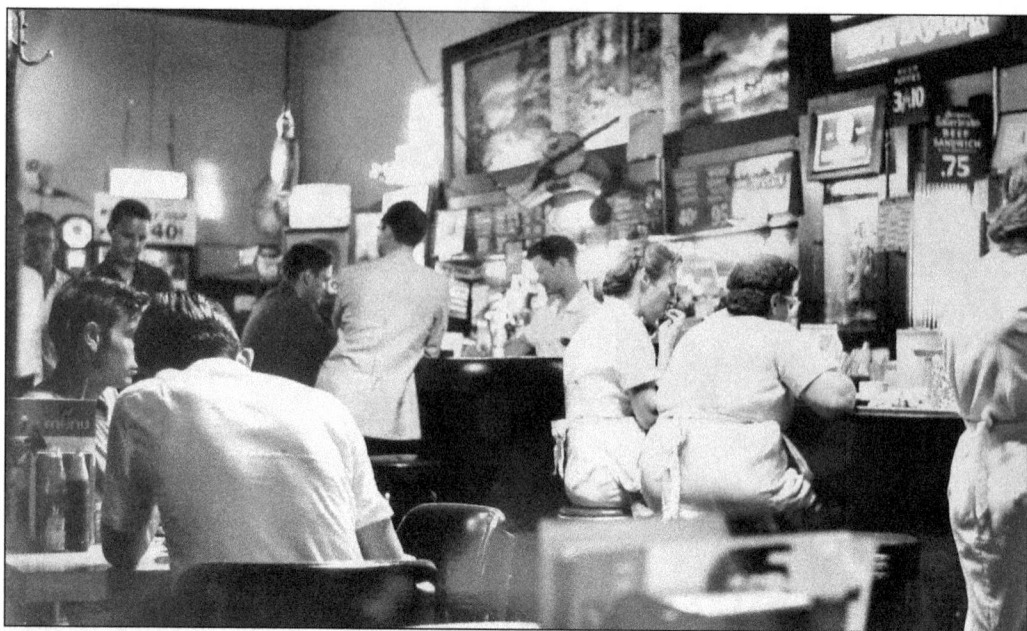

This photograph shows Eddie serving up some beer while several employees take a break at the counter. The restaurant always drew a large lunch crowd for such favorites as Berliner mett with sauerkraut, sauerbraten, Limburger on rye, and of course pig knuckles. Many of these dishes are from authentic German recipes brought to America by the Gerst family. (From the collection of Sam Hunt.)

This jacket was believed to be worn by William J. Gerst daily while he worked at the Gerst Haus. Gerst died November 13, 1968, but his daughter, Gene Gerst Ritter, continued to operate the Gerst Haus with her husband, Eugene Ritter. (From the collection of Sam Hunt.)

DRINKING HORN

GRANDFATHER'S MUG

MENU

HARVEST FESTIVAL

This drawing of the first Gerst Haus hangs in both the Nashville and Evansville Gerst Hauses today. This appeared in the Nashville *Tennessean* in 1970 when it was announced that the restaurant would be moving due to the urban renewal project downtown. (From the collection of the Gerst Haus, Nashville, Tennessee.)

This photograph shows the Gerst Haus as it appeared in its second location at 228 Woodland Street. The restaurant stood in this location from 1970 until 1998, when it had to close for the construction of the Tennessee Titans' football stadium. (From the collection of the Gerst Haus, Nashville, Tennessee.)

Pictured here is a much older Shorty pouring a fishbowl of beer at the second Gerst Haus. The Ritters sold the Gerst Haus restaurant and its historical memorabilia to the Chandler brothers in the late 1980s. The Chandlers continue to operate the Gerst Haus restaurants today, as well as other restaurants and bars in Nashville and Evansville. (From the collection of the Gerst Haus, Nashville, Tennessee.)

The bar, bar back, and many of the interesting advertising items that where at the first restaurant were transferred over to the new one. This photograph shows two of the wildlife lithographs, the "Gerst on Tap" porcelain sign, and the "Old Original" Gerst neon sign. (From the collection of the Gerst Haus, Nashville, Tennessee.)

For decades, draft beer has been served in "fishbowls," which are heavy glass goblets. In this photograph, the bartender, Jack Roberts, grabs two fishbowls in order to pour a few draft beers for thirsty patrons. The painting of Donau that once hung in William Gerst's office can be seen behind the bar in this photograph. (From the collection of the Nashville Room, Tennessee Public Library.)

The oompah and polka entertainment has been a huge success within the Nashville community. It became so popular that even the polka king himself, Frankie Yankovic, attended the Gerst Haus. This photograph shows Johannes van Dijk, accordion player for the Musik Meisters (one of the house bands that plays at the Gerst Haus) greeting Frankie Yankovic (bottom left) and his guests. (From the collection of the Johannes van Dijk.)

This photograph shows the Musik Meisters during a set at the Gerst Haus. Pictured on the left is the band's front man, Robert Granger, also known as Mongo. He would encourage the patrons to get involved by doing the chicken dance, among other things. The band's leader, Karen Yatuzis (center), sings as well as playing the accordion and keyboards. (Courtesy of the Gerst Haus, Nashville, Tennessee.)

A Great American Beer...Brewed in the European Tradition

Gutes Bier und wahres Wort

Füllen u. leert

GERST YOUR THIRST

The Chandler brothers went to the Evansville Brewing Company to have Gerst Haus Premium Amber formulated after Gerst's Old Amber of the early 1950s. The new beer became so successful that it was decided in 1992 to bottle the product and market it as Gerst Amber, as it was renamed, throughout Tennessee and Indiana. (From the collection of Scott R. Mertie.)

Evansville Brewing Company brewed Gerst Amber up until it declared bankruptcy and later closed in 1997. The Pittsburgh Brewing Company purchased the brands owned by Evansville Brewing Company the following year. The Chandlers decided to continue serving Gerst Amber, so they contracted with Pittsburgh Brewing Company to brew it. Although Gerst Amber is available on draft, it is no longer available in bottles for retail purchase. (From the collection of Scott R. Mertie.)

Gerst Amber neon signs were distributed by the Evansville Brewing Company to stores that carried Gerst Amber. Although it is only 15 years old, this neon has become a highly collectible item. (From the collection of Scott R. Mertie.)

Evansville Brewing Company issued quite a few promotional items when it was marketing Gerst Amber in Indiana and Tennessee. These beer mugs were issued to various bars that carried the brand on draft or in bottles. On the top is a heavy pewter mug with Gerst Amber molded into the side. The other is a glass mug with the Gerst Amber logo painted on it. (From the collection of Scott R. Mertie.)

Pictured here is a beer mat (coaster) with the Gerst Haus Premium Amber Beer logo on it. The fishbowl, borrowed from the Gerst Haus, contains matchbooks with the Gerst Amber logo. (From the collection of Scott R. Mertie.)

Pictured are six examples of tap handles that have been used at the Gerst Haus since it starting serving beer under its own name. The two tap handles to the right and the lower-middle handle are early Gerst Haus Premium Amber handles. The other three were used in later years after the name was changed to Gerst Amber. (From the collection of Scott R. Mertie.)

The Gerst Bavarian Haus opened in Evansville, Indiana, in 1999 after the closing of the Nashville location the previous year. It occupies the century-old Heidt and Voelker hardware building located at 2100 West Franklin Street. Initially it made sense to open a restaurant in Evansville, as the locals were already familiar with the brand because Gerst Amber was made there. Unfortunately, the Evansville Brewing Company closed while plans were being made to open the Gerst Haus in Evansville. The Chandlers decided to move forward, and the restaurant has been a success in Evansville's west side ever since. (From the collection of the Gerst Haus, Evansville, Indiana.)

The Gerst Bavarian Haus in Evansville cannot be missed as one drives down Franklin Street. The painting on the building is approximately 30 feet high and can be seen from several blocks down the street. (From the collection of the Gerst Haus, Evansville, Indiana.)

Advertising the Gerst Bavarian Haus, this old Porcelain sign from the 1940s hangs outside above the front door. The sign is double sided, and neon has been attached to accent the Gerst Beer. (From the collection of the Gerst Haus, Evansville, Indiana.)

The much anticipated third Nashville Gerst Haus opened at 301 Woodland Street, just across the street from its previous location, in August 2000. The opening caught the attention of the local media as it had been several years since Nashville had a Gerst Haus. This location still has the same menu as the previous locations, so patrons can get their fill of pig knuckles, kraut balls, and schnitzel. (Photographs taken by Scott R. Mertie.)

A Taste of Germany

Featuring Our Very Own *Gerst Amber* On Tap

25 Draughts

Live Oompah Band
Friday & Saturday Nights

Open 7 Days For Lunch & Dinner

Coldest Beer in Nashville

Fresh Fish Daily
and Great Salads

Outdoor Patio

Coldest Beer In Town

And of course...
Our Classic German Dining Menu

Gerst Haus
Since 1891

301 Woodland St. • 244-8886 (Across from The Coliseum)

This advertisement lets the public know that the Gerst Haus is open again and is back with its traditional German oompah band and Gerst Amber beer on tap. This newest rendition of the Gerst Haus features a large selection of imported German beers as well as American micro-brewed beers. (From the collection of Scott R. Mertie.)

Kimberly Holn, bar manager, has worked at the Gerst Haus for several years. In the photograph below, she has just poured a Gerst Amber in the ever-popular fishbowl. Notice that the bar back is the exact same as in the pictures of the first and second Gerst Haus. (Photograph by Scott R. Mertie.)

The new Gerst Haus still has the same bar and bar back that were at the first and second locations. On the walls hang the beautiful Gerst Girl lithographs, along with the painting of Donau. Photographs of the two previous locations are hung in frames around the booths of the restaurant. In this photograph, the four wildlife lithographs can be seen hanging over the bar. (Photograph by Scott R. Mertie.)

Six

MODERN BREWING
IN NASHVILLE

In the 1980s, craft beer, which is made in small batches and not mass-produced, began to become popular in the United States. Nashville's first brewery since the 1954 closing of the William Gerst Brewing Company opened in 1988, and later several brewpubs opened in the 1990s. This label is for a Three Treads Porter, a craft beer brewed by the Nashville Brewing Company, the same brewers at Blackstone Restaurant and Brewery. The label was designed with an old-world theme and educates the consumer on the history of the porter style. (From the collection of Scott R. Mertie.)

The Bohannon Brewing Company was founded by Lindsay Bohannon in 1988 and was Tennessee's original microbrewery. The brewery was located on Second Avenue, on the same spot where the Crossman and Drucker brewery once stood in 1859. The building that housed the brewery was built in 1888 as a warehouse for the Charles Nelson Distillery. By the mid-1990s, Bohannon opened a restaurant at the brewery, calling it Market Street Brewery and Public House in honor of the street's original name. (Photograph taken by Denise Huffines.)

This nut brown ale was one of the most popular beers brewed by the Bohannon Brewing Company. (Photograph by Scott R. Mertie.)

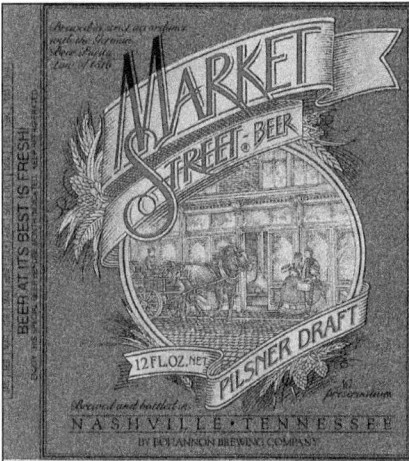
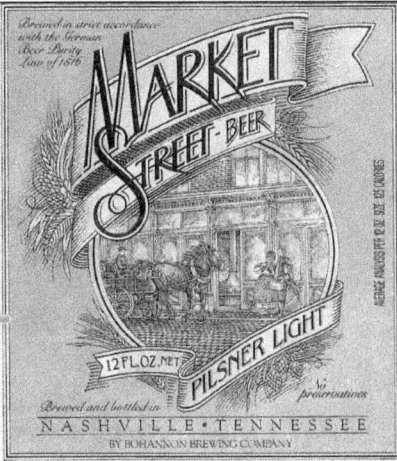
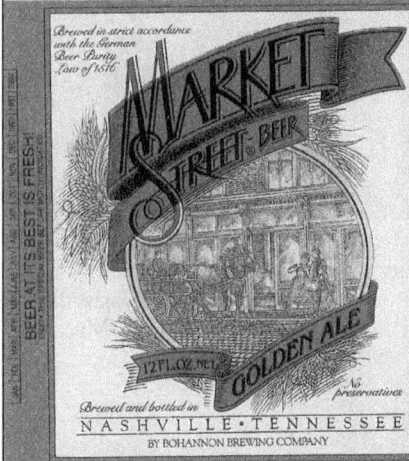
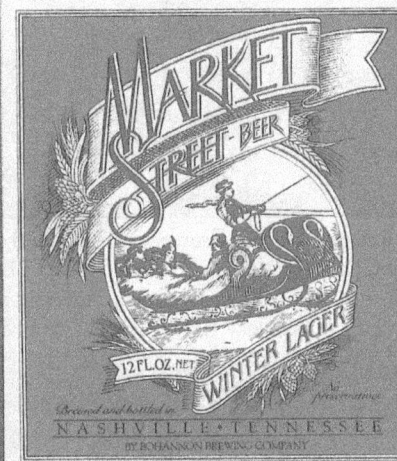

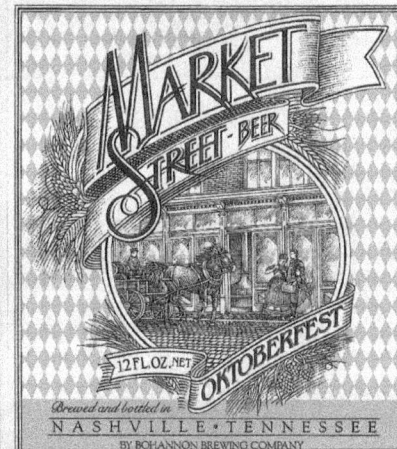

Although Bohannon brewed classic styles such as the brands pictured here, several flavored beers were also brewed and the bottled versions became quite popular in the Nashville area. Two of these styles were Bohannon's Vanilla Cream Ale and Blackberry Wheat. For various reasons, the brewery ceased production in January 2004, but the restaurant remains open. (From the collection of Scott R. Mertie.)

Blackstone Restaurant and Brewery was opened on New Year's Eve 1994 by restaurateurs and beer enthusiasts Stephanie Weins and Kent Taylor. They recruited Dave Miller, known for craft brewing in St. Louis, to come to Nashville to be their brewmaster. Blackstone became Nashville's first official brewpub (a brewery that also acts as a restaurant). (Photograph by Scott R. Mertie.)

Blackstone always has six beers on tap, plus one cask-conditioned ale. The four beers that are always on the menu are Chaser Pale (a German-style ale called Kölsch), Nut Brown Ale (a classic British-style ale), Red Springs Ale (an American amber ale), and St. Charles Porter (a British brown porter). Seasonal beers, such as Oktoberfest and oatmeal stout, are served on the other two taps throughout the year. (From the collection of Scott R. Mertie.)

After several years of operation, production increased, and Travis Hixon was hired to assist Dave Miller in the brewing process. Travis (left) and Dave are shown here standing in front of Blackstone's 15-barrel mash tun and brew kettle. (Photograph by Scott R. Mertie.)

In 2004, Blackstone began bottling and selling their two most popular brands, Chaser Pale and Nut Brown Ale, in Middle Tennessee. The beer is brewed in a much larger facility in Maryland, although it is not considered a "contract beer" since Miller and/or Hixon personally oversee the brewing process on-site. Blackstone may be opening a production brewery in Nashville in the near future. (From the collection of Scott R. Mertie.)

Boscos Nashville Brewing Company opened in 1996 in Hillsboro Village. This brewpub was an extension of its sister brewpub in Memphis, which opened several years earlier. The two-story brick building that Boscos occupies once housed the neighborhood five-and-dime store. (Photograph by Scott R. Mertie.)

Boscos is best known for its Boscos Famous Flaming Stone Beer, which is a traditional German-style stein bier. Stones are heated in wood-fired ovens and added during the brewing process to create a unique caramelized flavor. Other regular beers include Bombay IPA (a hoppy Indian pale ale), Germantown Alt (a malty, German ale), London Porter, and Isle in the Skye Scottish Ale. (From the collection of Scott R. Mertie.)

Boscos uses promotions, such as their Cellarman contest and the Mug Club, to attract and retain customers. A drawing is held daily during happy hour, and the winner gets to be the cellarman for the day or tap a keg of cask-conditioned ale. Once a year, the winners are brought together for a grand prize drawing for a trip to the Great American Beer Festival in Denver. Members of the Mug Club enjoy discounted beer rates in their own personalized mug and VIP status to various parties throughout the year. (From the collection of Scott R. Mertie.)

This photograph shows brewmaster Fred Scheer overseeing the boiling wort in the brew kettle. Fred was born and raised near Munich, Germany. He was trained in chemistry and later brewing and worked in several breweries in Germany. He later came to the United States where we worked for Pabst and several microbreweries in Michigan and Colorado before coming to Boscos. (Photograph by Scott R. Mertie.)

Big River Grille and Brewery Works opened in 1997 in downtown Nashville, just across the street from where the Silver Dollar Saloon was once located. Because of its proximity to downtown attractions, Big River is a popular destination for tourists. (Photograph by Scott R. Mertie.)

This photograph shows brewmaster Lance Roy preparing to pump the hot wort from the brew kettle to a fermentation tank. The brew house is uniquely located in the middle of the restaurant, completely surrounded by glass. (Photograph by Scott R. Mertie.)

NASHVILLE STEAMER GOLDEN ALE

One of Big River's most popular beers is Nashville Steamer, a golden ale. This beer combines honey malt with liberty hops, which provides consumers with a well-balanced and refreshing ale. Sweet Magnolia is an American brown ale, which is also very popular. Other brands include Southern Flyer Light Lager (American lager beer), Sixteenth Avenue Pilsner (traditional German lager with Hallertauer hops), Thick Brick Ale (a medium-bodied English ale), and Iron Horse Stout (a British-style stout). (From the collection of Scott R. Mertie.)

("Award Winning") SWEET MAGNOLIA AMERICAN BROWN ALE

123

Yazoo Brewing Company is Nashville's newest brewery, opened in October 2003. Owned and operated by Linus Hall, this microbrewery occupies the building that was once was home the historic Marathon Motor Works from 1910 to 1914. Hall initially started brewing four styles of beer and marketed his beer as a contract brew to area restaurants. (Photograph by Scott R. Mertie.)

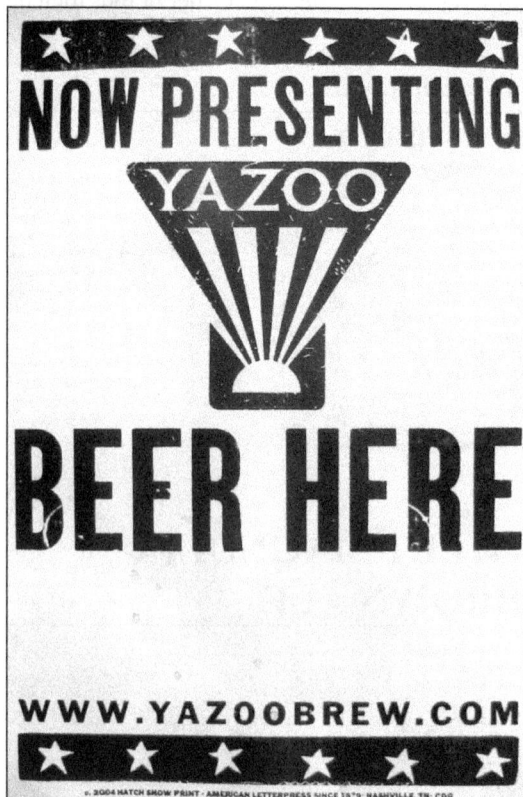

Linus Hall has done a wonderful job utilizing retro-advertising to promote his beers in the Nashville market. Yazoo's beers are on tap in many restaurants in Middle Tennessee, including the Gerst Haus. Signs like the one pictured can be seen hanging in bars throughout town. (From the collection of Scott R. Mertie.)

Yazoo currently has six beers that can be enjoyed at the brewery's taproom or area bars and restaurants. These brands include Amarillo Pale Ale, Dos Perros (two dogs), Onward Stout, Hefeweizen, Yazoo ESB (extra special bitter), and Sly Rye Porter. Lisa Wasilko, of JJ's Market on Broadway, is seen in this photograph pouring a pint of Yazoo's Hefeweizen, a popular wheat beer that won the gold medal for its category in 2004. (Photograph by Scott R. Mertie.)

Yazoo began bottling its beer in 2005 and is now distributing to grocery stores and specialty beer stores throughout Nashville and surrounding areas. The two brands currently being bottled are Dos Perros and Amarillo Pale Ale. The labels were designed by Hall's wife and business partner, Lila. (From the collection of Scott R. Mertie.)

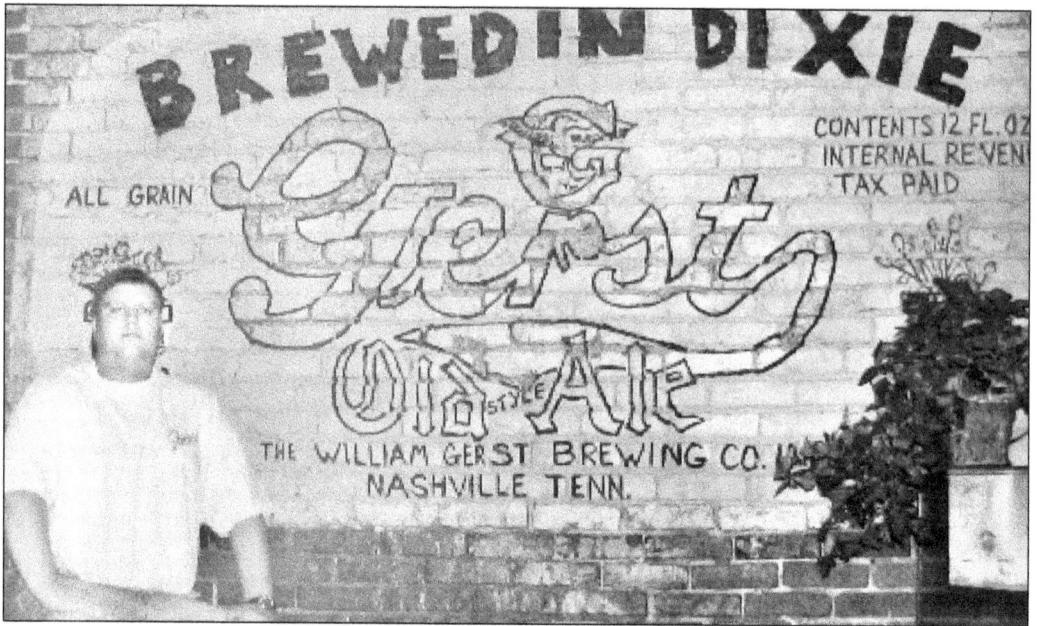

Here the author is pictured in front of a replica Gerst mural in Blackhorse Pub and Brewery. The main dining room has murals of all of the popular Tennessee beer labels from the first half of the 20th century. Blackhorse is located in a historic downtown building about 45 minutes outside of Nashville in Clarksville, Tennessee. (Photograph taken by Candy Mertie.)

Since 2003, Nashville has played host to the annual Music City Brewer's Festival. This annual event is held on the last Saturday in July and allows beer enthusiasts to enjoy beer samples from the Nashville breweries, as well as from a variety of regional and national breweries. In addition to beer, food and entertainment are also prevalent during the day. In this picture, volunteer Shawn Cunningham, wearing his lederhosen, is pouring samples of Boscos' Famous Flaming Stone Beer for some thirsty patrons. (Photograph taken by Scott Mertie.)

The author is seen in this picture with a small section from the second Gerst Haus picked up during the demolition. Scott R. Mertie was born and raised in Ohio and has been living in Tennessee since 1992. Scott began picking up beer cans from the side of the road at the age of six and quickly became an avid collector. By the time Scott was a teenager, his passion grew to collecting all kinds of breweriana. While in college at the Ohio State University, his interest in the beer industry expanded to home brewing and the craft-beer revolution. Within a week of moving to Nashville in 1992, Scott visited the Gerst Haus for the first time. He was amazed with the vast amounts of breweriana displayed throughout the restaurant, which started his fascination with the William Gerst Brewing Company. When he's not attending breweriana events or brewing a batch of beer, Scott works as a healthcare consultant for a regional CPA firm. He lives in Brentwood, Tennessee, with his wife, Candy, and two dogs. (Photograph taken by Chance Blackwell.)

DISCOVER THOUSANDS OF LOCAL HISTORY BOOKS FEATURING MILLIONS OF VINTAGE IMAGES

Arcadia Publishing, the leading local history publisher in the United States, is committed to making history accessible and meaningful through publishing books that celebrate and preserve the heritage of America's people and places.

Find more books like this at
www.arcadiapublishing.com

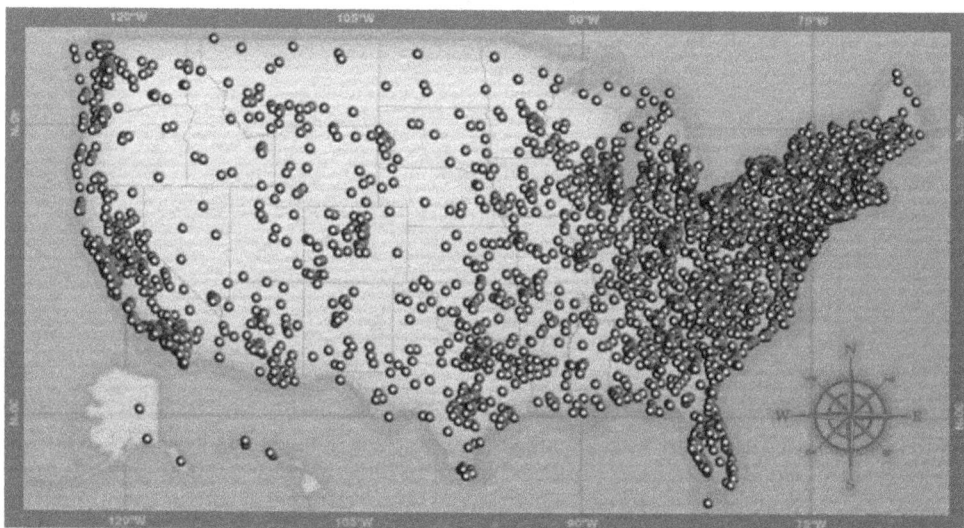

Search for your hometown history, your old stomping grounds, and even your favorite sports team.

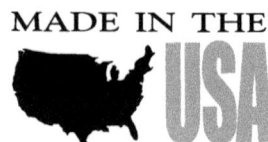